AMERICAN INQUISITORS

Other Transaction
Titles by Walter Lippmann

A Preface to Morals

American Inquisitors

Force and Ideas : The Early Writings

Liberty and the News

Public Opinion

The Method of Freedom

The Phantom Public

The Public Philosophy

AMERICAN INQUISITORS

WALTER LIPPMANN

With a New Introduction by
Ron Christenson

Transaction Publishers
New Brunswick (U.S.A.) and London (U.K.)

Third printing 2009

New material this edition copyright © 1993 by Transaction Publishers, New Brunswick, New Jersey 08903. Originally published in 1928 by The Macmillan Company.

This book is printed on acid-free paper that meets the American National Standard for Permanence of Paper for Printed Library Materials.

Library of Congress Catalog Number: 92-16068
ISBN: 978-1-56000-635-0
Printed in the United States of America

Library of Congress Cataloging-in-Publication Data

Lippmann, Walter, 1889-1974.
    American inquisitors /Walter Lippmann; with a new introduction by Ron Christenson.
        p.   cm.
Originally published: New York: Macmillan, 1928.
Includes bibliographical references.
ISBN 1-56000-635-8 (paper)
    1. Teaching, Freedom of—United States. 2. Modernism. 3. Fundamentalism. 4. Politics and education—United States. 5. Patriotism—United States.
    I. Title. LC72.2. L57   1992

371.1'04—dc20   92-16068
                                                                          CIP

CONTENTS

Contents

INTRODUCTION TO THE
TRANSACTION EDITION

American Inquisitors is Walter Lippmann's neglected, nearly forgotten gem. His biographers give it a slight glance in passing. Reviewers have mainly ignored it. Yet this short book, comprising his Barbour-Page Lectures at the University of Virginia in 1928, contains a succinct analysis of a basic dilemma of democracy. It is also a key to understanding Lippmann's own political principles.

The trials of John Scopes in Dayton, Tennessee, in 1925 and William McAndrew in Chicago in 1927 prompted Lippmann in his 1928 lectures to issue a warning against the threat political power presents to genuine education. In both cases those who presumed to speak for the majority—the Tennessee legislature and William Jennings Bryan in the Dayton case and Mayor William Hale (Big Bill) Thompson and the school board in Chicago—blew the bugle call of popular sovereignty. But *American Inquisitors* searches deeper than the dangers of the tyranny of democracy.

A TALE OF A TRIAL IN ONE CITY:
DAYTON, TENNESSEE

In January 1925, Representative John Butler wrote and introduced a bill in the Tennessee legislature that prohibited the teaching of evolution in all public schools, making it unlawful "to teach any theory that denies the story of Divine Creation of man as taught in the Bible, and to teach instead that man has descended from a lower order of animals." His bill soon became the locus of pressure. Some Baptist groups saw it as a club to use against their rivals, the Methodists. Most politicians realized the likelihood of campaign charges that, if they opposed the Butler bill, they did not believe the Bible. Speaker Lew Hill proclaimed, "Save our children for God!" and the bill swept through the legislature, 71 to 5 in the House and 24 to 6 in the Senate. By March 31 Governor Austin Peay signed it into law, although he hedged his signing with the qualification that he did not think the act would put teachers in any jeopardy, interfere with teaching, or even be enforced. "Nobody believes that it is going to be an active statute."[1]

In early May, George Rappelyea, a coal engineer and friend of biology teacher John Scopes, read in the Chattanooga newspapers that the American

Civil Liberties Union (ACLU) would finance a test case of the Butler law. Rappelyea convinced his friend Scopes that he should be the test: "It's a bad law. Let's get rid of it. I will swear out a warrant and have you arrested. . . . That will make a big sensation. Why not bring a lot of doctors and preachers here? Let's get H.G. Wells and a lot of big fellows." The ACLU responded to a wire from Rappelyea that it would support the defense with "financial help, legal advice and publicity."[2]

On May 7, Scopes was arrested and charged with using a textbook by George Hunter, *Civil Biology*, the standard, state-approved textbook, which contained such sentences as: "We have now learned that animal forms may be arranged so as to begin with the simple one-celled forms and culminate with a group which contains man himself." In New York Roger Baldwin announced for the ACLU that if necessary the case would be taken to the United States Supreme Court "to establish that a teacher may tell the truth without being thrown in jail." In Pittsburgh William Jennings Bryan announced that if the Tennessee officials agreed he would participate in the prosecution. He maintained, "We cannot afford to have a system of education that destroys the religious faith of our children."[3] By 7 June, Clarence Darrow, fresh from Chicago's sensational Leopold and Loeb murder case, was named chief counsel in John Scopes' defense.

The ballyhoo, as Lippmann calls it, took off when the trial opened in Dayton on 10 July, 1925. More than a hundred reporters lined the press tables and a radio hook-up made the trial the first ever to be broadcast. "My gavel," Judge John T. Raulston declared, "will be heard around the world."[4]

Because Lippmann's concern is with the ballyhoo surrounding the trial, we need not here consider the details beyond noting several highlights. The captivating speech of the trial was delivered by neither Bryan nor Darrow but by Dudley Field Malone. Although he had once served under Bryan when Bryan had been secretary of state, in the Scopes trial Malone became the life of the defense when he made an eloquent plea for educational freedom. He rejected Bryan's declaration that he would conduct a "duel to the death" against evolution because, as Malone put it, "there is never a duel with the truth."[5] Instead, he pleaded, adults should give "the next generation all the facts, all the available data, all the information that learning, that study, that observation had produced. . . . Make the distinction between science and theology. Let them have both."[6]

After Judge Raulston refused to allow scientists to be sworn as witnesses, the defense called a surprise witness, William Jennings Bryan. Darrow's cross-examination of Bryan dealt with Bryan's claim that the Bible must be understood literally. He asked Bryan about Eve and the serpent, Noah and the flood, Jonah and the whale, as well as whether Joshua made the sun stand still and if Bryan realized what the consequence of that might be. On the next day the judge struck Bryan's testimony from the record, and, after closings and judge's instructions to the jury, the jury spent nine minutes in deliberation before returning a verdict of guilty.

One irony of the trial is that, in spite of the brouhaha, Scopes had never taught evolution. Scopes had missed some class hours because he had been coaching football. Evolution was among the missing lessons. The students whom Scopes had to round up and persuade to testify against him could not remember whether or not they had ever studied evolution, and Scopes was afraid that if he took the stand he would have to admit his innocence and see Dayton lose its opportunity to be put on the map.[7]

Bryan died a few days after the end of the trial. Scopes' conviction was overturned by the Tennessee Supreme Court in 1927 because, contrary to statute, the judge, not the jury, set the fine of $100. This denied the ACLU its opportunity to appeal to the United States Supreme Court and possibly have the anti-evolution law declared unconstitutional. Ironically, the Tennessee law became instead a model for other states which enacted anti-evolution statutes.

Because his wife, Faye, was having surgery, Lippmann was not able to attend the Scopes trial. I doubt that he would have attended the trial even if he were able. Lippmann was not a reporter but an editor and commentator. He seldom sought to be on the scene. The journalist who did attend and whose reports, more than any other's, made the Scopes trial a sensational media event was H.L. Mencken. Unlike Lippmann with his detachment and determination to be fair, Mencken carried a full ideological agenda to the trial. Mencken gave the Scopes trial its popular name—the monkey trial—and, in league with Darrow, sought to use the trial to discredit Bryan. "Nobody gives a damn about that yap schoolteacher," Mencken told Darrow. "The thing to do is make a fool out of Bryan."[8] That, in turn, would undermine Puritanism in America and demonstrate that democracy is rule by the ignorant, the weak, and the inferior. For all of Lippmann's criticism of democracy, he never gave in to Mencken's cynical Nietzschean and Social Darwinist critique.

THE TALE OF A TRIAL IN A
SECOND CITY: CHICAGO

Because it had no Mencken-style ballyhoo, the trial of William McAndrew, unlike Scopes', is now forgotten. In 1927-28, however, the McAndrew trial received clamorous attention from the Chicago mayor, Big Bill Thompson. Lippmann saw the sensationalism in both trials and properly parallels their basic issues. Both trials challenge us, in the end, to think about our theory of liberty. Because McAndrew's is not known while Scopes' is legendary, more must be said in background about the McAndrew trial.

William McAndrew was the Chicago superintendent of schools, appointed by Mayor William E. Dever and forced out by Mayor Thompson over the issue of patriotic history. Dever had a term as a crime fighting, good government mayor. Big Bill Thompson's terms were best known for the ease of relations with civic leaders of the stripe of Al Capone. Dever, seeing chaos developing in the public schools, sought educational quality. McAndrew, who had been principal at Chicago's Hyde Park High School before going to New York as an assistant superintendent, returned to Chicago as Dever's reform superintendent.

McAndrew's program included a 100 percent mastery of reading, writing, spelling, punctuation, and arithmetic. He also reduced the number of school holidays and stood against any ward heeler who sought to influence teacher hiring. When he dissolved teachers' councils, which met on classroom time and presented a challenge to the authority of principals, the Chicago Teachers' Federation called him an autocrat.[9] The major opposition to McAndrew came from Jack (Iron-Handed) Coath, a school board member with close ties to Thompson. McAndrew was perceived as a foreign—namely, English—influence because of the history textbooks he had approved for use in the Chicago schools. In Coath's judgment they were un-American.

When Thompson threw his hat into the ring in the 1927 campaign, one of the two planks of his platform was "to run Superintendent McAndrew out of town." The other was to make Chicago a wide-open city. Capone and his business associates especially approved of the second, but the first was a better vote getter when it went under the Thompson slogan, "America First!"

McAndrew, Thompson claimed, was his main issue. McAndrew represented the influence of King

George. "Treason-tainted school textbooks," Thompson later wrote, "were a big issue in the Chicago mayoral campaign last Spring. I exposed the vicious pro-British, un-American propaganda in the school histories which were in the Chicago public schools with the approval of Superintendent William McAndrew, who had been imported from New York by the Dever Administration through the influences exerted by Professor Charles E. Merriam of the University of Chicago, and members of the English-Speaking Union. I showed how in many histories Revolutionary war heroes were defamed when mentioned, and how many were treated with the silence of contempt by being omitted entirely from the school histories."[10] Thompson demanded that more American patriots of Polish, German, and Irish descent be included and celebrated in the school textbooks. That his selection of these ethnic groups happened to coincide with his Chicago Republican Party machine coalition is probably no accident. He had a fine instinct for political correctness.

Thompson's campaign attack on McAndrew had its parallel in his attack on the Chicago Public Library. When Thompson had been informed that the library contained books soaked with British propaganda and anti-American sentiments, he appointed his friend, Sport Herrmann, to investigate the library. Herrmann announced that he would burn every library book which was pro-British. "There must be thousands of propaganda books in the library system. I'll hunt them out and when I find them I'll burn them on the lake shore." Although Herrmann received resolutions of praise from several organizations—American Association for the Recognition of the Irish Republic, several German-American groups, and the Illinois Ku Klux Klan, which further urged that Thompson add Catholics and Jews to the list—most groups either condemned or satirized Herrmann's effort. The Chicago Methodist Ministers' Conference passed a mock resolution of sympathy for George III and George V for "the terrible ordeal through which they have been called to pass by an outrageous asininity." The Cook County Jail Warden, Edward Fogarty, as the official hangman, announced that he would refuse to burn books. When Edward Bohac, a lawyer, filed a suit to obtain an injunction to restrain book burning, both Thompson and Herrmann denied that they planned a literary pyre on the shores of Lake Michigan. [11]

Herrmann did bag four books that he had been told were seditious, including Alfred Bushnell Hart's *The American Nation,* which had been dedicated to Theodore Roosevelt but Herrmann insisted had been "dictated by King George." Her-

rmann told reporters that he had not found the
time to read them but that he would turn them
over to the Patriots' League "and let them mark the
passages they think are pro-British. Then we'll have
something to go on." In the end the issue faded
when the yachting season opened and Sport
Herrmann spent time on the lake shore, but only
with his boat. Three years later, it should be
mentioned, he and a business partner contributed
$250,000 to the library for books. [12]

McAndrew's trial was preceded by a five-month
investigation chaired by former congressman John
J. Gorman. The Gorman Report was issued on 30
August, 1927, amid headlines proclaiming "GOR-
MAN ASSURES MAYOR 'BRITISH SCHOOL
PLOT' IS PROVED." "The sinister alterations in a
score of American school histories," the Gorman
Report maintained, "by which our annals are
perverted, our heroic fathers defamed and their
ideals and achievements grossly distorted to the
children, obviously could not have occurred by
mere coincidence. There is in each of these
histories a clearly defined motive, sometimes
definitely stated designs, which reflect the fruition
of the seeds planted by the Rhodes scholarship, the
Carnegie Foundation, and the English-Speaking
Union." The report made several books objects of
concern: Arthur Meier Schlesinger, *New Viewpoints*

in American History; Everett Barnes, *Short American History*; Willis Mason West, *The Story of the United States*; the Hart textbook cited by Herrmann as well as another which he co-authored and dedicated to George Washington. It singled out, however, the textbook by David Muzzey of Columbia University, *American History* (1925). Any person connected with Muzzey's book was at once suspected of conspiracy. The book had escaped notice six years earlier when the Patriot League of New York conducted a textbook purification. "Immediately secret, potent influences," the Gorman report pointed out, "caused William McAndrew, then an assistant superintendent of that city to be appointed head of the textbook division of the New York school system. Promptly under the McAndrew administration, additional Muzzey histories flooded the schools."[13] When McAndrew was brought into the Chicago schools, the Muzzey circulation grew by leaps and bounds.

"From my examinations of the historical textbooks now in use in the public schools of Chicago," Gorman concluded, "I am firmly of the opinion that the purification of our histories and the dissemination of American patriotism can be successfully attained only by the compilation of an entirely new history."[14] The new School Board chair, Iron-Handed Jack Coath had already announced that a pamphlet which would correct the "erroneous and pro-British" statements in history texts was being prepared and that several thousand copies would be distributed when school opened in September.[15]

Coath, in his new position as the head of the school board, took up the attack on McAndrew. In the newspapers Coath characterized McAndrew as an outsider bringing in the British influence, "an importation from New York." Yet McAndrew had taught and had been a principal in Chicago for twenty-five years before taking the New York position. McAndrew pointed out that he had first come to Chicago in 1886 but that Coath arrived in 1902. "He says I'm not a Chicagoan. What is a Chicagoan anyway? Must one remain in the city twenty-five consecutive years, or can one go away and return and still keep his standing as a Chicagoan?"[16] Coath would also serve as the chair of the tribunal, the school board, which was obligated by Illinois law to try the Superintendent before it could dismiss him. Coath announced that McAndrew was ousted on 29 August, and the trial, or more accurately, hearing, began on 29 September, 1927.

The legal issue in the trial was insubordination, concerning McAndrew's support of 283 teachers in a suit to restrain the school board from replacing them with civil service clerks. In mid-August McAndrews gave testimony that the work of "extra teachers" was "predominantly educational" because they supervise teaching, advise parents, and otherwise perform the work of a teacher. McAndrews maintained that his testimony was "not hindering the board—it was helping it." Only if the superintendent was viewed as a mere executive officer to carry out the board's policy, McAndrews maintained, would his testimony in the teachers' suit be considered lese majesty, that is, treason. [17]

If insubordination was the legal agenda, the Gorman Report and history books constituted the political agenda in the trial. The indictment contained sixteen counts of improper conduct by McAndrew, most of them derived from the Gorman Report: recommending history textbooks "tainted" with pro-British propaganda which omitted the names and exploits of "many foreign and native born heroes"; causing the picture "Spirit of '76" to be removed from the walls of schools "for the purpose of perverting and distorting ideals and patriotic instincts of school children in Chicago"; refusing to recommend that children donate money to the reconditioning of the ship, Old Ironsides; entering into a conspiracy with Charles E. Merriam and others "to destroy love of America in the hearts of children by encouraging teachers to attend special classes at the University of Chicago at which a textbook was used which pictured George Washington as a rebel and a great disloyalist"; plus demonstrating "insubordinate, insolent, domineering" conduct toward the board. After McAndrew pled not guilty to the charges, his attorney, Francis X. Busch, moved that Coath was unfit to preside because of public statements prejudicial to McAndrew. [18]

The board voted consistently six to five, with some votes six to four (when one member abstained), against McAndrew. Thompson called upon the five who supported McAndrew and "unpatriotic histories" to resign if "they were not in a conspiracy with the king of England." When they refused to resign, he called them "blue noses." Thompson summed up his attitude toward the trial, and presumably that of Coath and his supporters, by claiming, "Those who stand for American ideals are going to run Chicago's school affairs. They represent the will of the people. . . . I have no private war with the king of England, but I want him to keep his nose out of our schools."[19] In January 1928 the trial came to an end, and in March McAndrew was officially ousted. McAndrew filed a libel suit against Thompson but dropped it in 1929 when a judge overturned the board's ruling and declared that McAndrew had been neither insubordinate nor unpatriotic. McAndrew's favorite story concerned Thompson, who, when asked which King George he opposed, George III or George V, replied, "What? Are there two of them?"[20]

AMERICAN INQUISITORS AND AMERICAN DEMOCRACY

In the light of the trials of John Scopes in Dayton, Tennessee and of William McAndrew in Chicago, Lippmann challenged his generation to think about its theory of liberty and democracy, asking itself whether or not the theory was adequate. Lippmann found it lacking. *American Inquisitors* distills the arguments surrounding the two trials into five concise dialogues. Each dialogue explores a dilemma and leads to the next until the fifth places us in a position of having to continue the dialogue ourselves. The dialogues get to the heart of political theory.

The first two dialogues are three-cornered and take place on Olympus. In the first one Bryan asserts the dogma of majority rule, Jefferson the dogma of freedom of the mind, and Socrates urges a reexamination of all principles. Bryan is the populist, Jefferson the liberal, and Socrates the teacher of both. After these positions are clearly established in the first dialogue, Lippmann employs the second to raise the issue of the meaning of freedom in a democracy. Bryan's confidence in the people and Jefferson's in reason are put to the test by Socrates who suggests that most people have no time for thought. "Ideas are of no use to them unless they provide means of dealing with the things that worry them. . . . They want ideas which they can count upon, sure cures, absolute promises, and no shilly-shallying with a lot of ifs and per-hapses" (45). This leads toward a question about the meaning of freedom. "I was free because I wanted so little," Socrates concludes. "You were free because you wanted nothing more. But people are never free who want more than they can have. Their wants create worries, their worries create prejudices, their prejudices demand guaranties, and under freedom of thought nothing is guaranteed" (48-49).

The third and fourth dialogues are set in Dayton and Chicago, the cities of the two trials. In Dayton a Modernist and a Fundamentalist square off against each other, and in Chicago a Scholar and an Americanist argue. In neither dialogue does Lippmann create caricatures in order to discredit them. Lippmann puts challenging insights into the mouths of the Fundamentalist and the Americanist. They, like the Modernist and the Scholar, present plausible arguments. Out of the dialogues come some basic choices: Does commitment to the community come before the inquiring mind? Or, does the search for truth precede identity? These are issues Plato and Aristotle must have argued. Lippmann places them before us in modern times, and we can easily update them to our own decade. The Americanist, for instance, maintains that only the correct attitude will determine what is true history. For the Americanist, this means that a politically correct approach is necessary before the truth of history will be discovered. In the 1920s political correctness may have meant patriotism. Today it might mean the opposite. A floating patriotism or anti-patriotism will remain flexible. So will the truth.

The final dialogue is between Socrates and a teacher, that is between the exemplary teacher and a conscientious one. It moves the issues away from conformity and rebellion toward a situation in which teachers know what they are doing and why, where they are going and how fast, what they are searching for and when to face the consequences of the truth. Socrates tells the teacher that both Washington and Lincoln defied the constituted authorities and were later justified: "That which brave men do with wisdom lesser men make rules to justify" (110). Lippmann concludes with a basic principle of his theory of liberty and democracy: "Whoever the sovereign, the program of liberty is to deprive him of arbitrary and absolute power" (111).

The dialogues left some critics dissatisfied with the direction of Lippman's thought and others confused. Harold Lasswell thought that Lippmann had forsaken his earlier scientific attitude, presumably manifest in *Public Opinion*. Concerning *American Inquisitors*, Lasswell observed that "the world may be richer in maxims of political ethics if Lippmann continues in this vein; it surely will be poorer in understanding the obscure processes which are working upon the body politic, and which in times past he has helped to illuminate."[21] Fellow journalist Gerald W. Johnson, on the other hand, seems to have reached an opposite misunderstanding, prompting Lippmann to write to him:

> Now I feel pretty certain that I didn't make myself clear, because you seem to think that my book is an argument for the omnicompetence of the scientific spirit. That's just what it isn't. It is the most convincing demonstration I could make of the inadequacy of scientific spirit, and for proof of that I refer you again to the

> dialogues between the Fundamentalist and
> the Modernist, and between the Scholar
> and the Americanist. In fact, the chief
> emphasis of the book is directed against
> the dry, thin rationalist. [22]

If the dialogues in *American Inquisitors* aim at anything, they are directed at the need to wrestle with basic questions. Dogmas of both religion and science endanger such questioning.

Political correctness in any age is what Lippmann calls servility of mind. His critique of such servility is reflected in the book's title as much as in his commentary. William Jennings Bryan stood for making majority rule a fundamental dogma as much as he stood for biblical fundamentalism. Big Bill Thompson, likewise, stood for majority rule and the dogma of patriotism. The consequences of either undermine freedom. Society's floating opinion can be as tyrannical as its rigid orthodoxy. Literal and unbending interpretations of either Scripture or history are as restricting as an imperative ideology. A servility of the mind permits an easy manipulation by those who hold power. Absolute power and the pretense of sovereignty follow.

American Inquisitors is the distillation of Lippmann's early writings and the germ of his later works. His rebuke of popular sovereignty is a theme throughout all his books. But his early writings offer a suggestion similar to Plato's, that democracy cannot by itself move outside Plato's Cave. The public is a prisoner in the cave. In *Public Opinion* (1920) Lippmann argued "that democracy in its original form never seriously faced the problem which arises because the pictures inside people's heads do not automatically correspond with the world outside." Jefferson's democratic theory and modern socialism, he maintained, ignored the difficulties of a complex society and assume "that somehow mysteriously there exists in the hearts of men a knowledge of the world beyond their reach."[23] Lippmann's solution, like Plato's, was that representative government needs a panel of experts to fit the reality of the world to the pictures in our heads. The public cannot make sound judgments, Lippmann suggested, because it "will arrive in the middle of the third act and will leave before the last curtain, having stayed just long enough perhaps to decide who is the hero and who the villain of the piece."[24]

While Lippmann never demonstrated despair over democracy, his early writings express doubt about the potential, on its own, for creating a reasonably civilized society. Democracies are haunted, he concluded in *The Phantom Public*, "by this dilemma: they are frustrated unless in the laying down of rules there is a large measure of assent; yet they seem unable to find solutions to their greatest problems except through centralized governing by means of extensive rules which necessarily ignore the principle of assent. The problems that vex democracy seem to be unmanageable by democratic methods. In extreme crises the dilemma is presented absolutely."[25] In such frustration popular government is likely to accept what Lippmann called the "cult of the second best."[26]

The dogma of majority rule, which he saw personified in William Jennings Bryan and Big Bill Thompson, is based on a mythology which, ironically, is Jefferson's:

> Beginning with a theory based on the vision of a very simple village community where everyone knew everybody else's character and affairs, and inspired by a high sense of human equality, the democrat found himself in an unmanageable civilization. No man's wisdom seemed to be great enough for the task. A somewhat more mystical wisdom was necessary. But about the steadiness of the supply of that wisdom he still had inner doubt. Then

came the doctrine of interests to relieve the tension. It was said, apparently on the highest scientific authority, that all men instinctively pursued their interests; that their reason need not be dealt with because it was a mere pretext for their wishes; and that all you had to do was to probe for the interests of the people, and you were in touch with reality.[27]

This "sleight of hand" in popular mythology led to majority tyranny and demagoguery. The consequence was not anticipated by Jefferson, but it derives from his theory. What happens to be interesting, as measured by public opinion, becomes the measure of the public interest and of reality itself.

In short, Lippmann in *American Inquisitors* brings Jefferson's original vision together in dialogue with Bryan's popular sovereignty, finding both inadequate, the former because it does not fit modern complexity and the latter because it is a form of domination.

Lippmann's later writings, from *A Preface to Morals* (1929) to his *Public Philosophy* (1955), move his thinking toward a response with more religious depth. His apprehension about the inadequacy of Jeffersonian democracy and his warning about the dangers of majority tyranny never abated. Perhaps they intensified with his concern for what he called "the acids of modernity" and the breakdown of public authority when "Whirl is King."[28] But the questions and ideas Socrates raises in the dialogues in *American Inquisitors* suggest that the answers to the problems of democracy lie in recovering a public sense of commitment. He concludes *American Inquisitors* by expressing an anxiety that, with the breakdown of belief in the modern world, "we shall lack the support and guidance of a philosophy" (117). But the danger lies in the society's potential for improvising compensations for lost certainty and guidance. A substitute civil religion may bring tyranny.

A more explicit answer to the questions raised in the dialogues prompted by the Scopes and McAndrew trials is found in *A Preface To Morals* where Lippmann pointed out that when modernity dissolved the dogmas of popular religion, a "high religion" must be accepted. This means a "religion of the spirit" which is "an almost exact reversal of the worldling's philosophy," a call for disinterestedness and reason, for the inner life and what might be called a genuine civil religion. In his 1937 book, *The Good Society*, Lippmann ruled out any notion of popular sovereignty and called for a modern natural law. The free and ordered society is impossible "unless in community there is a general willingness to be bound by the spirit of a law that is higher and more universal than the letter of particular laws."[29] Lippmann seems to have moved from Plato's answers to Aristotle's. By his 1955 *Public Philosophy*, which he began writing in the 1930s, Lippmann continued the same theme he initiated in *American Inquisitors*, presenting a clearer response to the dilemma of democracy. The guide in politics and morals is not the will of any sovereign group, such as a majority, but is discovered in those "traditions of civility" by which we rule ourselves, that "second and civilized nature" which Socrates sought.[30]

A friend once criticized Walter Lippmann for "always trying to dredge up basic principles," which would not do for a newspaper. A newspaper, the critic said, is like a bugle. It has only four notes, and the most a newspaper can do is choose sides in a fight and fight as hard as it can, although its writers may secretly wish the nature of the fight were different. "You may be right," Lippmann responded. "But damn it, I'm not going to spend my life writing bugle calls."[31]

Ron Christenson
Gustavus Adolphus College

Notes

1. Ray Ginger, *Six Days or Forever? Tennessee v. John Thomas Scopes* (Oxford: Oxford University Press, 1958), 7.
2. Ibid., 20.
3. Ibid., 21.
4. Ibid., 103.
5. Lawrance M. Bernabo and Celeste Michelle Condit, "Two Stories of the Scopes Trial: Legal and Journalistic Articulations for the Legitimacy of Science and Religion," in *Popular Trials: Rhetoric, Mass Media, and the Law*, ed. Robert Hariman (Tuscaloosa: University of Alabama Press, 1990), p. 69.
6. Ginger, *Six Days*, 138.
7. Ibid., 180; Bernabo and Condit, *Popular Trials*, 58.
8. Garry Will, *Under God: Religion and American Politics* (New York: Simon and Schuster, 1990), 109.
9. Lloyd Wendt and Herman Kogan, *Big Bill of Chicago* (Indianapolis: Bobbs-Merrill, 1953), 235.
10. William Hale Thompson, "Shall We Shatter the Nation's Idols in School Histories?" *Current History* XXVII (February, 1928): 619. See also William Hale Thompson, "Are We Victims of British Propaganda? *The Forum* (April, 1928): 503-509.
11. Wendt and Kogan, *Big Bill*, 289-291.
12. Ibid.
13. *Chicago Daily Tribune*, 31 August, 1927, 1.
14. Ibid., 1-4.

15. Ibid.
16. Ibid., 23 August, 1927, 3.
17. Ibid., 21 August, 1927, 3.
18. Ibid., 30 September, 1927, 6.
19. Ibid., 1.
20. Wendt and Kogan, *Big Bill,* 302.
21. Harold Lasswell, review of *American Inquisitors, American Journal of Sociology* 34 (1928-1929): 559.
22. To Gerald W. Johnson, 18 May, 1928. *Public Philosopher: Selected Letters of Walter Lippmann,* ed. John Morton Blum (New York: Ticknor and Fields, 1985), 220.
23. Walter Lippmann, *Public Opinion* (New York: Macmillan, 1960), 30-31.
24. Walter Lippmann, *The Phantom Public* (New York: Harcourt, Brace, 1925), 65.
25. Ibid., 189-190.
26. Walter Lippmann, "Second Best Statesmen," in *Men of Destiny* (New York: Macmillan, 1927), 229. Originally published in 1922.
27. Ibid., 235.
28. Walter Lippmann, *A Preface to Morals* (Boston: Beacon Press, 1960), 208-210.
29. Walter Lippmann, *The Good Society* (New York: Grosset & Dunlap, 1926), 335.
30. Walter Lippmann, *The Public Philosophy* (Boston: Little, Brown, 1955), 139.
31. Charles Wellborn, *Twentieth Century Pilgrimage: Walter Lippmann and the Public Philosophy* (Baton Rouge: Louisiana State University Press, 1969), 9.

PREFACE

This is a book made up of lectures delivered
at the University of Virginia by invitation of
President Alderman and the faculty committee
acting for the Barbour-Page Foundation.

There are, as I see it, two things which a lec-
turer can do. He can speak with authority on
some subject which he has mastered. But I
am not an authority on any subject and I know
only too well that I have not mastered this one.
Or the lecturer can explore and inquire, aiming
to open up the subject rather than to conclude
upon it. That is what I have done here. And
that is why at the most contentious and difficult
points in the inquiry I have resorted to the
Socratic dialogue.

The subject of these lectures is the pre-
dicament of the modern teacher under popular
government during the conflict over religious
fundamentalism and over patriotic tradition.
The same problem with variations presents
itself to all whose business it is to popularize
ideas. If any reader feels that I might more

profitably have discussed the problem as it presents itself in the office of a newspaper, my excuse is that I am too close to that phase of the problem to speak about it objectively and disinterestedly. No sensible physician ever attempts to make an important diagnosis on members of his own family.

W. L.

March, 1928.

Chapter I

New Phases of an Ancient Conflict

I—New Phases of an Ancient Conflict

I. BALLYHOO

As one whose business it is to write about public affairs, I have often been made to feel like a man at the theatre who forgets where he is and shouts at the hero to beware of the villain. For of late it has been our mood in politics to regard ourselves as the spectators at a show rather than as participants in real events. At a show well bred people do not hiss the villain. They enjoy the perfection of his villainy and recognize that he is necessary to the show.

We have become very sophisticated. We have become so sophisticated that we not only refuse to mistake make-believe for reality, but we even insist upon treating reality as make-believe. We are so completely debunked that we have almost persuaded ourselves that all beer is near-beer and that every battle is a sham battle.

That part of the American people which likes to think of itself as the civilized minority has insisted for some years now that no intelligent man can afford to be caught holding the illusion that any public event really matters very much. For public affairs are the serious occupation only of dunderheads, cowards, trimmers, frauds, cads on the one hand, and of opponents of prohibition, motion picture censorship, and the obscenity laws on the other. They assure us that in the main public affairs are insufferably dull. Taxation is dull. The maintenance of peace is dull. Imperial responsibilities are dull. Everything is dull,—if you treat it responsibly. But if you are a man of wit and discernment you will not treat anything responsibly. You will not expect to be edified. You will manage to be entertained. Having convinced yourself that nothing matters much, having forgotten that it is fully as difficult to govern a state as to write an essay, you will find that the spectacle of democracy in action is a glorious farce full of captivating nonsense.

I do not know whether newspaper writers belong to the civilized minority or not. But I do know that they have never been so thoroughly convinced as they are today that the measure of events is not their importance but their value as entertainment. This is the mood of the people. When my friend Mr. Mencken says "I enjoy democracy immensely. It is incomparably idiotic, and hence incomparably amusing," the democracy replies, or would if it could express itself, "You said it, old man. Everybody ought to have a sense of humor and enjoy himself. We have enjoyed ourselves mightily with half a dozen gorgeous murders, beauty contests, and the inner secrets of a lot of love nests." For the booboisie and the civilized minority are at one in their conviction that the whole world is a vaudeville stage, and that the purveyors of news are impresarios whose business it is to keep the show going at a fast clip. It is still customary to record the conventionally important affairs of state. But they are like the prescribed courses for freshmen, things which you have to pass in order to pass them by.

The real energies of the enterprising members of my profession have recently gone into the selection, the creation, the staging, and the ballyhooing of one great national act after another. Sometimes it is a sordid act. Sometimes, as in the Lindbergh idyll, it is a beautiful act. What matters is that it should never be a dull act. The technical skill which this requires is great. It is no easy thing to keep the excitement going with never a dull moment, and with intermissions just long enough for the audience to go out into the lobby for a breath of air. It is a new and marvellous profession, this business of entertaining a whole nation at breakfast. It is a profession which the older and more sedate editors look upon much as if they were deacons and had been asked to dance the Black Bottom.

2. DAYTON AND CHICAGO

Among the events on which the modern art of ballyhoo has been practised there are two at least which are not likely to be forgotten soon. The world laughed at them, but it has not yet laughed them off. For they are symbols and portents. I refer to the trial of John T. Scopes at Dayton and to the trial of William McAndrew at Chicago. With your permission I propose to discuss these two cases as marking a new phase in the ancient conflict between freedom and authority.

This place is an appropriate one surely to such a discussion. For the University of Virginia is a temple erected by Jefferson to the belief that the conclusions reached by the free use of the human reason should and will pre-

vail over all conclusions guaranteed by custom
or revelation or authority. For this boldness
Jefferson was, as you know, fiercely attacked as
seditious and godless, not only by the Thomp-
sons and the Bryans of his day, but by many of
the important leaders of thought. The first
appointment to the faculty of this University
aroused a storm of protest in the legislature
because the Board of Visitors wished to appoint
Dr. Cooper, a man who had been prosecuted
under the Sedition Law, and was accused as
well of being a Unitarian. A century has
passed. Legislatures are still ready to be
aroused as they were against Dr. Cooper. But
Jefferson's theory has become the acknowledged
principle of education in all modern communi-
ties. There are no longer educated men any-
where who would openly venture to challenge
the principle that there is no higher loyalty for
the teacher and the scholar than loyalty to the
truth.

And yet this principle is under attack today
in all sections of the country. The attacks are
made by churchmen and by patriots in the name
of God and country. The attack of the church-
men is aimed chiefly at the teaching of the bio-
logical sciences, the attack of the patriots at
the teaching of history. I need hardly tell

you that Dayton and Chicago are exceptional
only in the amount of attention they have re-
ceived. They happened to lend themselves to
the art of ballyhoo. They are not unique.
They are merely episodes of a wide conflict
between scholarship and popular faith, between
freedom of thought and popular rule, which
irritates American politics with deep discords.
The spirit of the Tennessee Statute against the
teaching of the theory of evolution is not con-
fined to Tennessee. The purpose behind it
has been carried into effect in many American
communities either by statute, by adminis-
trative ruling, or by the self-denying ordinances
of frightened educators. The threat of legis-
lation like that in Tennessee is almost as effec-
tive as the actual legislation itself, and that
such a threat exists as a determining influence
on education in many parts of this country, no
one, I think, will deny. The same holds true
of the patriotic inquisition which is typified by
Mayor Thompson's crusade against the text-
books of history used in the Chicago schools.
Mayor Thompson did not start this crusade.
He has merely carried on a little more spectacu-
larly the zealous work which others had begun.
There are few communities, therefore, in which
there has not been some sort of inquisition

recently to find out if the teachers are as religious as Dr. John Roach Straton or as patriotic as Mayor Hylan of New York, Mayor Thompson of Chicago, and Mr. William Randolph Hearst.

These assaults upon the freedom of teaching have been supported by the ignorant part of our population, the spokesmen of these new inquisitions have often been mountebanks, and invariably they have been ignoramuses. As a result, educated men have been disposed, partly because they were sincerely contemptuous, partly because they were prudent, to treat the whole matter as a farce which would soon break down through its own inherent absurdity. It is very easy to make light of the Chicago inquisitor who could not recall in the excitement of his patriotism whether it was Nathan Hale or Ethan Allen who regretted that he had only one life to give for his country. It is fairly funny to read that the Mayor of Chicago has drawn up a list of patriots of Polish, German, and Irish descent, who ought to be celebrated in the Chicago schools. But I am not so sure that it is possible to laugh all this off, and I am not so sure but that at the core of all this confusion there is not something of great importance which it behooves us to understand.

I am inclined to think that Dayton and Chicago are landmarks at which it is profitable to pause and ask ourselves whether the theory of liberty which we inherit is adequate. I do not find it adequate. My own experience as a controversial journalist during the last ten years has convinced me that while the intelligence and the wit of the community are opposed to these clerical and patriotic inquisitions, there exists no logically consistent philosophy of liberty with which to combat them. I am thoroughly persuaded that if Mr. Bryan at Dayton had been as acute as his opponents, he would have conquered them in debate. Given his premises, the logic of his position was unassailable. I am no less persuaded that the objects of Mayor Thompson's crusade could be stated in a way which would compel the respectful attention of every thinking man.

I know perfectly well that Mayor Thompson cannot state them in such a fashion. But I see no advantage in winning a cheap victory just because the opposition has a poor lawyer. I propose, therefore, to ignore as irrelevant all the superficial absurdities of the attacks on learning, to ignore the discreditable motives which sometimes confuse the issue, to ignore above all the squalid ignorance which surrounds these controversies, and instead to examine them sympathetically and dispassionately, not in their weakness and folly, but in their strength. I propose, if you please, to be the Devil's Advocate.

Need I remind you that the real title of that official is Promoter of the Faith?

3. A CURIOUS COINCIDENCE

I should like at the outset to invite your attention to a curious coincidence. I have before me a copy of Jefferson's Bill for Establishing Religious Freedom. This bill, as you know, was accepted in 1786 with a few unimportant changes by the General Assembly of Virginia. It has been called the first law ever passed by a popular assembly giving perfect freedom of conscience, and by common consent it is regarded as one of the great charters of human liberty. I have before me also the text of the bill which was passed by the General Assembly of the State of Tennessee on March 13, 1925, entitled An Act Prohibiting the Teaching of the Evolution Theory.

No two laws could be further apart in spirit and in purpose than these two. And yet at one point there is a strange agreement between them. On one vital matter both laws appeal to the same principle although they aim at diametrically opposite ends.   The Virginia statute says that "to compel a man *to furnish contributions of money* for the propagation of opinions which he disbelieves, is sinful and tyrannical."   The Tennessee statute prohibits "the teaching of the evolution theory in all the universities, normal and all other public schools of Tennessee, *which are supported in whole or in part by the public school funds of the State."* You will note that the Tennessee statute does not prohibit the teaching of the evolution theory in Tennessee.   It merely prohibits the teaching of that theory in schools to which the people of Tennessee are compelled by law to contribute money.   Jefferson had said that it was sinful and tyrannical to compel a man to furnish contributions of money for the propagation of opinions which he disbelieves.   The Tennessee legislators representing the people of their state were merely applying this principle.   They disbelieved in the evolution theory, and they set out to free their constituents of the sinful and tyrannical compulsion to pay for the propagation of an opinion which they disbelieved.   The late Mr. Bryan made this quite clear:

"What right," he asked, "has a little irresponsible oligarchy of self-styled intellectuals to demand control of the schools of the United States in which twenty-five millions of children are being educated at an annual expense of ten billions of dollars?"

Some time ago I pointed out this disturbing coincidence to a friend of mine who has devoted many years of his life to the study of Jefferson. After a few remarks about the devil quoting Scripture, he said that the coincidence shows how dangerous it is to use too broad a principle in justifying a practical aim. That of course is true. Jefferson, like other enlightened men of his time, believed in the separation of church and state. He wished to disestablish the church, which was then supported out of public funds, and so he declared that taxation for the propagation of opinions in which a man disbelieved was tyranny. But while he said 'opinions,' he really meant theological opinions. For ardently as he desired to disestablish the church, he no less ardently desired to establish a system of public education. He thought it quite proper to tax the people to support the public schools. For he believed that "by advancing the minds of our youth with the growing science of the times" the public schools would be elevating them "to the practice of the social duties and functions of self-government."

One hundred and forty years later the political leader who in his generation professed to be Jefferson's most loyal disciple, asked whether, if it is wrong to compel people to support a creed they disbelieve, it is not also wrong to compel them to support teaching which impugns the creed in which they do believe. Jefferson had insisted that the people should not have to pay for the teaching of Anglicanism. Mr. Bryan asked why they should be made to pay for the teaching of agnosticism.

4. DIALOGUE ON OLYMPUS

This was, I believe, a momentous question which we have been too busy to debate. But perhaps by this time, Mr. Jefferson and Mr. Bryan have met on Olympus where there is plenty of time. If they have, let us hope that Socrates is present.

SOCRATES: I have been reading your tombstone, Mr. Jefferson, and I see that you are the author of the Declaration of Independence, the Statute for Religious Freedom, and that you are the Father of the ·University of Virginia. You do not mention more worldly honors. It is evident that your passion was for liberty and for learning.

JEFFERSON: It was. I had, as I once said to Dr. Rush, sworn upon the altar of God eternal hostility against every form of tyranny over the mind of man.

SOCRATES: And this I believe is Mr. Bryan, three times the chosen leader of the party which you founded.

JEFFERSON: In a manner of speaking, yes.

SOCRATES: A disciple of yours?

JEFFERSON: You, too, had disciples, I believe.

SOCRATES: Yes, more than I care to remember. They often quarrelled. I shall not go further into that.

JEFFERSON: You were always kind.

SOCRATES: We shall see. I shall ask you a few questions.

BRYAN: Mr. Jefferson can answer them all.

JEFFERSON: I'm not so sure.

BRYAN: A good conscience can answer any question.

SOCRATES: I'm afraid then that I never had a good conscience.

BRYAN: It was good considering that you were a foreigner and a heathen.

SOCRATES: You, too, were accused of being

a heathen. Were you not, Mr. Jefferson, ac-
cused of being an enemy of religion?

BRYAN (interrupting): That is a foolish
question. You may not know it, Mr. Socrates,
but he was twice President of the United States.

JEFFERSON: I was denounced as an atheist
by many good people.

SOCRATES: Were you an atheist?

JEFFERSON: No, but I disestablished the
church in Virginia.

SOCRATES: On what theory?

JEFFERSON: I reflected that the earth was
inhabited by a thousand million of people, that
these professed probably a thousand different
systems of religion; that ours was but one of
that thousand; that if there were but one right,
and ours that one, we should wish to see the
nine hundred and ninety-nine sects gathered
into the fold of truth. But against such a
majority we could not effect this by force. I
said to myself that reason and persuasion are
the only practicable instruments. To make way
for these, free inquiry must be indulged; and
how could we wish others to indulge it while
we refused it ourselves?

SOCRATES: Had not every state in your day
established some religion?

JEFFERSON: That is true. I replied, with

some exaggeration I admit, that no two had
established the same religion. Was this, I
asked, a proof of the infallibility of establish-
ment?

SOCRATES: So you disestablished the church.

BRYAN: He did, sir, and thus proved his
sterling Americanism.

SOCRATES: You also, Mr. Bryan, believe in
the complete separation of church and state?

BRYAN: I do, sir, most certainly. It is
fundamental.

SOCRATES: Can it be done? . . . You look
surprised. I was merely wondering.

BRYAN: It has been done in America.

SOCRATES: I won't argue with you about
that. I should like to ask Mr. Jefferson some
more questions. For example: the church
which you disestablished had a creed as to how
the world originated, how it is governed, and
what men must do to be saved? Had it not?

JEFFERSON: It had.

SOCRATES: And according to the church this
creed was a revelation from God. In refusing
to pay taxes in support of the teaching of this
creed, you asserted, I suppose, that this creed
was not revealed by God?

JEFFERSON: Not exactly. I argued that
the validity of this creed was a matter for each

individual to determine in accordance with his own conscience.

SOCRATES: But all these individuals acting as citizens of the state were to assume, I take it, that God had not revealed the nature of the universe to man.

JEFFERSON: They were free as private individuals to believe what they liked to believe about that.

SOCRATES: But as citizens they could not believe what they liked?

JEFFERSON: They could not make their private beliefs the official beliefs of the state.

SOCRATES: What then were the official beliefs of the state?

JEFFERSON: There were none. We believed in free inquiry and letting reason prevail.

SOCRATES: I don't understand you. You say there were many people in your day who believed that God had revealed the truth about the universe. You then tell me that officially your citizens had to believe that human reason and not divine revelation was the source of truth, and yet you say your state had no official beliefs. It seems to me it had a very definite belief, a belief which contradicts utterly the belief of my friend St. Augustine for example. Let us be frank. Did you not overthrow a state religion based on revelation and establish in its place the religion of rationalism?

BRYAN: It's getting very warm in here. All this talk makes me very uncomfortable. I don't know what it is leading to.

SOCRATES: I don't either. If I did, I should not be asking questions. What is your answer, Mr. Jefferson?

JEFFERSON: I'll begin by pointing out to you that there was no coercion of opinion. We had no inquisition.

SOCRATES: I understand. But you established public schools and a university?

JEFFERSON: Yes.

SOCRATES: And taxed the people to support them?

JEFFERSON: Yes.

SOCRATES: What was taught in these schools?

JEFFERSON: The best knowledge of the time.

SOCRATES: The knowledge revealed by God?

JEFFERSON: No, the best knowledge acquired by the free use of the human reason.

SOCRATES: And did your taxpayers believe that the best knowledge could be acquired by the human reason?

JEFFERSON: Some believed it. Some preferred revelation.

SOCRATES: And which prevailed?

JEFFERSON: Those who believed in the human reason.

SOCRATES: Were they the majority of the citizens?

JEFFERSON: They must have been. The legislature accepted my plans.

SOCRATES: You believe, Mr. Jefferson, that the majority should rule?

JEFFERSON: Yes, providing it does not infringe the natural rights of man.

SOCRATES: And among the natural rights of man, if I am not mistaken, is, as you once wrote, the right not to be compelled to furnish contributions of money for the propagation of opinions which he disbelieves, and abhors. Mr. Bryan, I think, disbelieves and abhors the opinion that man evolved from a lower form of life.

BRYAN: I do. It is a theory which undermines religion and morality.

SOCRATES: And you objected to being taxed for the teaching of such an opinion?

BRYAN: I most certainly did.

SOCRATES: And you persuaded the representatives of a majority of the voters in one state to forbid this teaching in the schools they were compelled to support.

BRYAN: It was an outrageous misuse of public funds.

SOCRATES: May I ask whether you meant that nobody should be taxed to support the teaching of an opinion which he disbelieves, or whether you meant that the majority shall decide what opinions shall be taught.

BRYAN: I argued that if a majority of the voters in Tennessee believed that Genesis was the true account of creation, they had every right, since they pay for the schools, not to have the minds of their children poisoned.

SOCRATES: But the minority in Tennessee, the modernists, the agnostics, and the unbelievers, also have to pay taxes. Do they not?

BRYAN: The majority must decide.

SOCRATES: Did you say you believe in the separation of church and state?

BRYAN: I did. It is a fundamental principle.

SOCRATES: Is the right of the majority to rule a fundamental principle?

BRYAN: It is.

SOCRATES: Is freedom of thought a fundamental principle, Mr. Jefferson?

JEFFERSON: It is.

SOCRATES: Well, how would you gentlemen compose your fundamental principles, if a majority, exercising its fundamental right to rule, ordained that only Buddhism should be taught in the public schools?

BRYAN: I'd move to a Christian country.

JEFFERSON: I'd exercise the sacred right of revolution. What would you do, Socrates?

SOCRATES: I'd re-examine my fundamental principles.

5. WHO PAYS THE PIPER CALLS THE TUNE

That is what I should like to attempt in these lectures. The greater part of the American people must of necessity be educated in public schools. These schools are supported by taxation and administered by officials who derive their authority from the voters. The question is: shall those who pay the piper call the tune?

It may be that to many among you these questions will seem speculative and remote. You may feel that I am making too much of the spectacles at Dayton and Chicago, and that I am wrong in taking them as symbols and portents of great significance. May I remind you, then, that the struggles for the control of the schools are among the bitterest political struggles which now divide the nations? Wherever there is a conflict of religious sects, you will find that the public schools are one of the chief bones of contention. It has been so in Canada for generations. It is so now in Mexico. In every country of Europe where there are national minorities, there is bitter dispute over the public schools. It is inevitable that it should be so. Wherever two or more groups within a state differ in religion, or in language and in nationality, the immediate concern of each group is to use the schools to preserve its own faith and tradition. For it is in the school that the child is drawn towards or drawn away from the religion and the patriotism of its parents.

The reason why this kind of conflict is relatively unfamiliar to us is that America has been until recently a fairly homogeneous community. Those who differed in religion or in nationality from the great mass of the people played no important part in American politics. They did the menial work, they had no influence in society, they were not self-conscious, and they had produced no leaders of their own. There were some sectarian differences and some sectional differences within the American nation. But by and large, within the states themselves, the dominant group was like-minded and its dominion was unchallenged.

But in the generation to which we belong a multitude of circumstances have conspired to break up this like-mindedness of the American people. The children and the grandchildren of the new immigration have come of age, have prospered, and have begun to assert a powerful influence in public life. Great cities have been founded which act, as cities always do, to dissolve the customs and beliefs which were nurtured in rural and provincial society. The United States has become an empire and a world power: its thought is fertilized and infected by all the winds of doctrine. There is no longer a well-intrenched community, settled in its customs, homogeneous in its manners, clear in its ultimate beliefs. There is great diversity, and therefore, there are the seeds of great conflict.

It is quite natural, then, that this generation should have witnessed the spectacles at Dayton and Chicago. It is natural too that they should have caused so much excitement. For this is the first generation which has realized that it is divided within itself about religion and about national destiny. A generation ago John T. Scopes would probably not have thought of teaching evolution in Tennessee. Or if he had, no one would have noticed the implications of such teaching. Or if the implications had been noticed, he would have been disciplined as a matter of course, and that would have been the end of it. But today the division of opinion between fundamentalists and modernists has become acute owing to the increasing strength of the modernists. Because both sides were so representative, the struggle at Dayton interested everybody. So it is with the Thompson crusade in Chicago. A generation ago American history was universally taught as an exercise in piety and patriotism. But within our time criticism and skepticism have succeeded in shaking the whole legendary creed of patriotism, and, in the chaos which has followed, a variety of patriotic sects have appeared each contending that it alone expresses the true American patriotism.

If I read the signs rightly, we are at the beginning of a period of intense struggle for the control of public education. There is no longer a sufficient like-mindedness in most American communities to insure an easy harmony between the teachers and the mass of their fellow citizens. I shall not attempt to enumerate all the different groups actually or potentially in conflict. But there is, for example, a conflict between fundamentalists and

modernists which has the profoundest bearing
on the future of scientific inquiry in many parts
of the West and South; there is a latent and un-
resolved conflict in the North and East between
Catholics and Protestants, in which the ex-
tremists among the Catholics are demanding a
share of the school funds for their parochial
schools, and the extremists among the Protes-
tants are demanding a state monopoly of educa-
tion which would abolish the parochial schools.

There is a kind of war within the schools
between the militarists and the pacifists which
comes to a head every so often in rows about
military training, in inquisitions as to the patri-
otism of teachers, in pleas that the schools
should emphasize the military virtues, or that
they should expound the horrors of war and
the blessings of peace. Chambers of Com-
merce also have taken a hand in the conduct of
schools, insisting that they be purged of what
is usually called bolshevism; and trades unions
have arisen to plead that the schools should
give more attention to the struggle of labor for
a better life. All the important national groups
of which we are composed have their eye on
the schools. The Anglophiles wish the schools
to teach that George III was only a miserable
German King, and not a good Englishman at

all. The Anglophobes wish it made very clear that George V still broods and plots at night over the misfortunes of George III. The unreconstructed Irish wish every school child to dwell long and portentously upon the fact that we have had two wars with Great Britain. Others among us like to dwell upon the fact that we have had no war with Great Britain for a hundred years, and shall have none ever again if we care for the future of civilization. The German societies would like a large place in the textbooks for von Steuben who drilled Washington's troops. The Polish societies would like a large place for Kosciusko. The professional Jews want the schools to stop reading The Merchant of Venice. And so it goes.

In fact, it almost seems as if there were hardly an organization in America which has not set up a committee to investigate the schools and to rewrite the textbooks. Apparently every organization feels itself eminently qualified to teach the teachers how to conduct the schools. There are I do not know how many schemes on foot for writing the ideal history book. That may surprise you. But in fact it is much easier than you think to write an ideal history. It is difficult to write a true history. But an ideal history is a history which

proves what you want it to prove. Almost
everybody, therefore, can write an ideal his-
tory. And almost everybody is writing one.

6. SERVILITY OF MIND

I am not prepared to say that this vast com-
motion around the schools is a wholly bad
thing. It creates excitement, and I should
rather see the teaching faculties excited because
they are under fire, than have them go com-
fortably and complacently to sleep. Then, too,
the ultimate effect of attack and counter attack
is to weaken the defences of authority. This
teacher or that may lose his job, but his opin-
ions are heard far more widely than if they
had been ignored. For it is a curious fact that
in the conflict between reason and authority,
the conflict itself is a victory for reason.
Authority is always on the road to defeat when
it has to appeal either to force or to reason.
It is secure only when it rests upon unques-
tioned habit. Inquisitions and heresy hunts are
therefore invariably the signs that reformation
and emancipation are under way.

There is, moreover, a considerable advantage
in compelling men to defend their opinions
against attack. It is not an unmixed advantage
by any means, but unless thought involved a

certain personal risk, it would be too tame for the human animal. It does add to the dignity of scholarship to remember that men have died not only for their gods and their flags, but for the freedom of the human mind. I have no personal desire, mind you, to be roasted alive for my opinions, and I know a fair number of martyrs who would not be half so happy if nobody persecuted them. But it does nobody any harm now and then to put his job, his income, his reputation, and even his automobile, in one pot on the table, and gamble them all on his convictions. It is a great protection against premature hardening of the arteries.

However, we need not fear, I think, that thinking will become too safe an occupation in our lifetime. It will remain an adventure for those who can think well. There is more danger in the constant threat of popular raids upon the schools. The bravest men are drawn off into mean squabbling and bickering which take more of their energy than the thing is worth. The less brave become dangerously prudent, not only in public but in their very souls, and a man who has become prudent in his own thinking has really ceased to think. There is no way of measuring what the public schools lose by the refusal of first-rate men to submit to the democratic inquisition and by the withering away of second-rate men who are terrorized by it.   But the loss is a big one, we may be sure.

Chapter II

Fundamentalism

II—Fundamentalism

I. THE TWO DOGMAS

The effect of this goading and poking from the outside has provoked Professor Carlton Hayes of Columbia University to say [1] that "the commissioners, superintendents, principals, etc.—the bureaucrats of the new education—discover that they must from the very nature of things, lead a kind of double life; they must be super-teachers, raising the standards of their schools, arousing the ambition of pupils, and setting an example of the highest idealism for their teachers; they must be also more or less servile representatives of the state, holding their teachers in check, guarding their pupils against radicalism and novelty, and generally maintaining such standards in the schools as reflect most faithfully the collective spirit of the taxpayers." In elementary state-schools under existing circumstances it hardly seems probable, he adds, that "the instruction will rise in character or quality much above the average

[1] In his *Essays on Nationalism.*

33

level of the prejudices of the whole state's citizenry."

Professor Hayes goes on to point out that some of these administrators are more Dr. Jekyll than Mr. Hyde, and that some are more Mr. Hyde than Dr. Jekyll, but that the best men must, if they aspire to a long tenure of office at a constantly augmenting salary, pay court to the prejudices of the taxpayers. Now it might be argued that the teaching profession could establish its independence if it were more prepared to stand up and fight. I believe that to be true. I believe that the body of educators have hardly realized the power they could exercise if they chose not to endure this perpetual bullying from ignoramuses.

Weakness always tempts the bully. Timidity always invites terrorism, and the teaching profession in America has in a very considerable degree brought upon itself the constant meddling of politicians and private snoopers. The profession has not valued its own dignity sufficiently to command the respect of the community. In Tennessee the university authorities turned tail and ran. They dismissed professors, cancelled lectures, and did their best to placate the inquisitors. What can be the effect of such conduct except to destroy the

morale of the whole body of teachers and to
incite the inquisitors to more extreme depreda-
tions? The teachers will be slaves if they act
like slaves. If they cower, they will be bullied.
The tragedy and the absurdity of the thing is
that they could so easily rally a following to
their support if they had the imagination to
realize how strong they are. Scattered, di-
vided, without leaders, demoralized by de-
serters—of course they are the victims of every
Meddlesome Matty now at large. But if they
chose to fight, if they chose to say that they
would not endure the intolerable indignities to
which they are subjected, they would very soon
command a new kind of respect in the nation.
They would also command a new kind of re-
spect among their pupils, for youth admires
courage more than any other virtue of man.
And the support of their own pupils would give
them immeasurable strength in every house-
hold, would set in movement a current of opin-
ion with which the inquisitors would have to
reckon.

Nothing can excuse or explain away spine-
lessness. But it is nevertheless true that there
are circumstances which weaken the spirit of
resistance. If educators in the public schools
have to lead a double life it is not due wholly

to personal timidity. It is due also to a confusion of mind. The teaching profession does not fight for its rights partly because there is great uncertainty as to what the rights are for which it ought to fight.

The effect of this uncertainty is to divide the minds of teachers, to bewilder them, to make them hesitate, and to drive them to seek undignified compromises. There is no clearly defined theory as to the status and the function of teachers in the public schools. They do not know clearly what they ought to fight for if they had the will to fight. They are stultified within their own spirits by their own lack of clear conviction.

It is not easy to work out a clear principle which will define the status and function of public school teachers. If you will recall the Dialogue on Olympus in last night's lecture, you will have concluded, I think, that the fundamental principles which we assume to be true are capable of being manipulated to the most surprising and contradictory results. It is possible, for example, to derive the Tennessee statute against evolution from one of the principles laid down in Jefferson's Bill for Establishing Religious Freedom. It is possible to derive justification for an established church from the very arguments used to disestablish a particular church.

Now at the heart of all this confusion we can, I think, distinguish two dogmas. Both of these dogmas are intricate and uncertain. The relation between them is even more intricate and uncertain. I refer to the Dogma of Freedom of Thought and to the Dogma of Popular Rule.

2. RESUMING ON OLYMPUS: CONCERNING FREEDOM

For the analysis of the implications of an idea we have no more convenient instrument than the Socratic dialogue. So with your permission I shall resume the Dialogue on Olympus at the point where it was broken off, last night.

JEFFERSON: You were saying, Socrates, that it would be well to examine these conflicting fundamental principles. I offer you as a beginning the principle laid down in my Notes on Virginia that reason and free inquiry are the only effectual agents against error.

SOCRATES: I believe that was not a new principle in your day?

JEFFERSON: Indeed it was not. You practised it yourself.

SOCRATES: So I did. There were others before me. I remember Protagoras who wrote a book *On the Gods,*—our gods, Mr. Bryan— which began: "Concerning the gods, I cannot say that they exist nor yet that they do not exist. There are more reasons than one why we cannot know. There is the obscurity of the subject and there is the brevity of human life." His books were collected and burned. Reason has never been popular.

JEFFERSON: It will prevail.

SOCRATES: What will prevail?

JEFFERSON: Reason will prevail. Galileo was sent to the Inquisition in 1616. But his book was taken off the Roman Index in 1835.

SOCRATES: So in this case it took only 219 years for reason to prevail. Why did it take so long?

BRYAN: The vested interests of the church were too strong for the people.

SOCRATES: I was put to death by vote of the people. The authorities would have been glad to have me escape. It was the triumph of democracy which finished me.

BRYAN: The people are sometimes misled.

SOCRATES: I dare say. The persecution of the Christians was rather provoked by the populace than desired by the authorities. The

Inquisition was very popular in its day. When the Pope and the Bishops relented, public opinion insisted upon the extermination of the heretics. The people are still like that down there below. It was, I think, the Great Commoner who led the last crusade against science. It is the newspapers of the larger circulations, which appeal to the great mass of the people, who are always smelling out treason in the schools.

JEFFERSON: And what do you conclude from all this?

SOCRATES: That the common people hate reason, and that reason is the religion of an élite, of great gentlemen like yourself.

BRYAN: Reason a religion? What do you mean?

SOCRATES: The common people have always known that reason is a religion. That is why they dislike it so violently.

JEFFERSON: Please speak more plainly.

SOCRATES: You advocated the use of reason and free inquiry. What for?

JEFFERSON: I said: "Give a loose to them, they will support the true religion by bringing every false one to their tribunal, to the test of their investigation."

SOCRATES: You said "their tribunal," the

tribunal of reason and free inquiry. I suppose these false religions, as you call them, also had a tribunal to which they summoned beliefs. What was that tribunal?

JEFFERSON: It was usually called revelation.

SOCRATES: And it was your theory that religions based on divine revelation should be investigated before the tribunal of human reason.

JEFFERSON: Yes.

SOCRATES: That God's Word should be tested by human words? What makes you so confident about human reason?

JEFFERSON: Many statements purporting to be revealed truth are demonstrably false. They can easily be disproved.

SOCRATES: Have not many statements based on reason turned out to be demonstrably false?

JEFFERSON: Their error has been exposed by reason and corrected by reason.

SOCRATES: So the difference between revelation and reason is that conclusions based on revelation cannot be corrected, but that conclusions based on reason can always be corrected.

JEFFERSON: That is right.

SOCRATES: Then you can never be sure that

a conclusion reached by reason is finally correct?

BRYAN: I demonstrated that at Dayton. I quoted several biologists who disagreed with Darwin.

SOCRATES: Did these biologists of yours say they had at last got the whole truth?

BRYAN: I don't think they did.

SOCRATES: So in this realm of reason you are never very sure of anything.

JEFFERSON: You must always keep your mind open for new evidence.

SOCRATES: Then if I understand you correctly a reasonable man is one who does not believe very firmly in his own reason.

JEFFERSON: He trusts his reason but he distrusts his conclusions.

BRYAN: This is getting very complicated.

SOCRATES: Well, it is complicated. Mr. Jefferson says that a man must believe that reason will give him the truth, but he must not believe too strongly that he has the truth when he has reasoned it out.

JEFFERSON: The work of reason is never finished.

SOCRATES: You wish men to believe in reason, but not in their reasoning at any particular moment. Is that it?

JEFFERSON: That is what is now called the scientific spirit.

SOCRATES: Does one not need faith to believe that reason, though never wholly successful, will at last conquer reality?

JEFFERSON: Sublime faith.

SOCRATES: Perhaps more faith than the ordinary man can feel?

JEFFERSON: What are you leading to?

SOCRATES: To an explanation of why the people reject reason though it has been consciously practised for two thousand years.

JEFFERSON: In the end they accept it. But it is a long and often a bitter struggle.

SOCRATES: Do they accept reason, or do they accept some conclusion at which reason has happened to arrive?

JEFFERSON: The scientific method is widely practised now.

SOCRATES: I grant you that. Reason has more devotees than it ever had before. But they are still a minority. I return to my question: is it a victory for reason if the people at last accept what they once regarded as dangerous heresy?

JEFFERSON: Not necessarily.

SOCRATES: Why not necessarily?

JEFFERSON: Because, as you so cunningly

pointed out, the conclusions reached by reason
are not final. By the time the people accept a
rational conclusion, it may no longer be ra-
tional. You would say, I suppose, that in
twenty-five years the mountaineers of Tennes-
see will swear by Darwin as violently as they
now swear at him.

BRYAN: I can say in this connection that
having had an opportunity to meet Mr. Dar-
win, it is evident that he is a kindly, patient,
and forbearing man.

SOCRATES: Yes, he will make an excellent
saint in the church which Clarence Darrow is
founding.

BRYAN: I didn't know that Mr. Darrow
was a churchman.

SOCRATES: Neither does Mr. Darrow. But
he is. When Mr. Darrow was younger than
he is today, scientific men found the hypothesis
of mechanism rather convenient. Mr. Darrow
has been teaching this hypothesis as gospel ever
since. He is very orthodox. It is a sad and
kindly religion which may have quite a vogue.

JEFFERSON: Does it persecute unbelievers?

SOCRATES: No. Mr. Darrow merely makes
them look foolish. But that hurts.

BRYAN: It does.

JEFFERSON: It would be better, as I told

Livingston at the end of my life on earth, if men learned to be less confident in the conclusions of human reason and to give more credit to the honesty of contrary opinions.

SOCRATES: You may remember that in the Laws of Manu it is enjoined on the Brahman that when his hair is white, and his skin is wrinkled, and he has looked on his son's sons, he shall turn his back on his home and his ordinary affairs, and withdrawing to the forest, shall devote the remainder of his days to meditation on the nature of the Infinite Being. When you wrote that to Livingston you had become the Sage of Monticello. You had turned your back on men.

JEFFERSON: I was consulted by all kinds of men to the end of my days.

SOCRATES: But you had forgotten what men are like if you thought they could endure it not to be confident of their conclusions.

JEFFERSON: Explain yourself.

SOCRATES: I feel that I am going to make a speech.

BRYAN: I shall like it.

JEFFERSON: I don't think I shall. I once told the president of a debating society that most oratory is an insult to an assembly of reasonable men, disgusting and revolting, instead of persuading. Speeches measured by the hour die with the hour.

SOCRATES: You rather enjoy quoting yourself.

JEFFERSON: No, these speeches are being put into my mouth.

SOCRATES: So are mine being put into my mouth.

BRYAN: Newspapermen like to put words into people's mouths.

SOCRATES: I do not complain. I am going to deliver my speech.

JEFFERSON: What were we talking about?

SOCRATES: I was about to explain why men cannot endure not being confident of their conclusions. And I was going to say that most men have no time for speculation. They have too many immediate worries. Ideas are of no use to them unless they provide means of dealing with the things that worry them. They feel insecure. They have to make a living, and they are constantly menaced by this and that, by drought and plagues, by wars and oppressions, by disease and death. An easy and tolerant skepticism is not for them. They want ideas which they can count upon, sure cures, absolute promises, and no shilly-shallying with a lot of ifs and perhapses. The faith of the people is always hard, practical, and definite. And that is why your religion of reason is not for them.

JEFFERSON: Because it denies them hard and fast conclusions on which they can rely absolutely?

SOCRATES: Yes. Have you ever stopped to think what it means when a man acquires the scientific spirit? It means that he is ready to let things be what they may be, whether or not he wants them to be that way. It means that he has conquered his desire to have the world justify his prejudices. It means that he has learned how to live without the support of any creed, that he can be happy, or at least serene, that he can be good, or at least humane, no matter what conclusion men may come to as to the origin of the world, or its plan, or its destiny. There are not many men of this sort in any age.

JEFFERSON: Utterly self-sufficient and disinterested men. Are they the only ones who can endure complete freedom of thought?

SOCRATES: They are the only ones. If a man has wants he must pay the price. If he wants gold and silver and big estates, he must want the kind of society in which it is possible for him to have these things. If he wants a

Scientific free Spirit:
the Obligation
to be strictly
objective

heaven of material well-being, he must want the kind of universe which will guarantee him such a heaven. It is only when he has ceased to care about the result that he can trust himself wholly to free inquiry.

JEFFERSON: Must a man then surrender everything if he is to be free?

SOCRATES: That was my conclusion. That is why I refused to flee to Thessaly when they left the prison door open for me. Had I run away in order to be able to eat a few more dinners, I should have been not a philosopher but the slave of my own stomach. Had I submitted to that, could I ever again have been sure that what I thought was the voice of reason was not in fact the rumbling of my own stomach?

JEFFERSON: Is freedom as difficult as you make it out?

SOCRATES: Not quite. I am now a legend devised by Plato to instruct mankind.

JEFFERSON: You mean that freedom may not require the complete renunciation of worldly desires?

SOCRATES: I mean that freedom may also be a matter of degree, and that men could enjoy a good deal of freedom if, while following their worldly desires, they did not think very highly of any of them.

JEFFERSON: But you said that most men were too preoccupied with the problem of living to look at life in this fashion.

SOCRATES: I adhere to that. And while mankind is thus preoccupied it will neither enjoy freedom itself nor tolerate too much of it in others. I was thinking of a considerable minority which now exists for the first time in the history of mankind, a class who no longer really need to worry about their safety or whether they can earn enough to live.

JEFFERSON: They may have other worries. Have you noticed the divorce courts down there?

SOCRATES: I am not a reformer. I was merely going to say that when the necessities of life are secure, a man can begin to be free. We in Athens founded our freedom on chattel slavery. So I think did you. You have got to found it on something. If they can do it with machines and organization and wise laws, well and good. The point is that a man can only begin to be disinterested when he has ceased to be hungry and uncomfortable and frightened. I was free because I wanted so little. You were free because you wanted nothing more. But people are never free who want more than they can have. Their wants create worries, their worries create prejudices, their prejudices demand guaranties, and under freedom of thought nothing is guaranteed.

3. DIALOGUE AT DAYTON

In the light of this analysis I should like to consider sympathetically the state of mind of a taxpayer in Tennessee who favored the passage of the so-called anti-evolution bill. That state of mind is fairly represented, I imagine, by a letter which appeared in the Knoxville News at the time of the controversy. The writer, after remonstrating with the newspaper for its failure to treat the law respectfully, concludes by saying: "The anti-evolution law prohibits the teaching that the world was created in any way except as set forth in Genesis. That is as it should be. Our children can now go to school without having all their faith and hope destroyed by science." [1]

MODERNIST: I don't see what difference it makes to faith and hope whether the world was created as set forth in Genesis or not. I could join you in insisting upon the moral truth of the Sermon on the Mount, but why do you insist upon the scientific truth of Genesis?

[1] Quoted in Maynard Shipley, *The War on Modern Science*, p. 220.

FUNDAMENTALIST: If I deny the teaching of Genesis, what assurance have I about the teaching in Luke, Matthew or Mark?

MODERNIST: The teachings of the Gospels are verified by the religious and moral experience of men. That is your assurance. But the teaching of Genesis runs counter to the knowledge of men.

FUNDAMENTALIST: This comes down to saying that I am to pick and choose what parts of the Bible I shall believe.

MODERNIST: Are you not a Protestant? Do you not believe in the right of private judgment?

FUNDAMENTALIST: Had you studied history a little more carefully you would not ask this question. You might examine Luther's views on Zwingli and on the Anabaptists.

MODERNIST: You mean that the right of private judgment was not a principle in Luther's teaching, but a method, provisionally adopted, for dealing with the authority of the Pope?

FUNDAMENTALIST: I do. For me the hope of salvation depends upon the authority of the Scriptures.

MODERNIST: The account of creation in Genesis has nothing to do with the promise of salvation.

FUNDAMENTALIST: You are quite wrong. It would make no difference if the Bible had said that the world was created in seven million years rather than in seven days or that man was descended from an ape. I could believe that as readily as I believe what I now believe. The important question is not what the Bible says about creation, but that the Bible says it. If the Bible is wrong about creation, how am I to know that it is not also wrong about salvation? I say to my children: You must not steal. . . . You must not lie. . . . You must keep the Ten Commandments. . . . You must follow the teachings of the Sermon on the Mount. . . . They say to me: Why should we do that? . . . I tell them it is God's will. They say to me: How do you know it is God's will? I reply: Because Scripture is the word of God divinely inspired. And then they say: Yes, but teacher says the Bible is wrong when it tells that woman was made from Adam's rib.

MODERNIST: Must your children then believe what is untrue in order that they may believe what is true?

FUNDAMENTALIST: I don't know that Genesis is untrue. Neither do you. You weren't there at the creation and neither was Darwin.

Your scientists are all at sixes and sevens, and none of them even pretends to know how the world came to be created.

MODERNIST: They know it could not have been created as set forth in Genesis.

FUNDAMENTALIST: They do, do they? Well, what if they do?

MODERNIST: Don't you want your children to respect the truth?

FUNDAMENTALIST: Indeed I do. That is just where I quarrel with modernism. It undermines the respect of my children for the truth. They learn a lot of half-baked theories about evolution in school, and then they come home disbelieving the whole religion and morality of their fathers, and recognizing no standards of conduct except their own wilfulness.

MODERNIST: You are going to ask me to believe that the whole of religion and of morality rests upon an old Jewish legend about the creation?

FUNDAMENTALIST: I am going to ask you to tell me what guarantee there is for religion and morality if you first reject the authority of the Catholic Church, as Protestants do, and then proceed to reject the authority of the Bible, as you modernists do?

MODERNIST: We do not reject the authority

of the Bible. We hold that it is profoundly inspired.

FUNDAMENTALIST: Is the whole Bible inspired?

MODERNIST: Not all of it. The Bible is a vast literature not all written at one time and by no means all of the same quality. The Bible is not a single book.

FUNDAMENTALIST: Then how do you know which parts of the Bible are, as you say, profoundly inspired?

MODERNIST: Those parts are inspired which are verified by the religious experience of mankind.

FUNDAMENTALIST: And how do you know that the religious experience of mankind is reliable? Do all modernists agree on what they will regard as the profoundly inspired parts of the Bible?

MODERNIST: There is some disagreement.

FUNDAMENTALIST: So that one modernist might call one part of the Bible inspired and another modernist might not.

MODERNIST: That is so.

FUNDAMENTALIST: Then perhaps you will tell me how I am to convince my children that any part of the Bible is inspired.

MODERNIST: You must enlarge their experience and train their judgment. Then they can decide for themselves.

FUNDAMENTALIST: They are to decide for themselves what is moral and immoral?

MODERNIST: They must learn to be guided in their decisions by the accumulated wisdom of the race.

FUNDAMENTALIST: Guided by it. But not bound by it?

MODERNIST: It is impossible to lay down absolute rules which will be valid in all cases.

FUNDAMENTALIST: So we have come to the conclusion that it is impossible to know for certain what God's will is. It is equally impossible to know for certain what the so-called wisdom of mankind is. Each youngster, therefore, is, under your system, to face the temptations and the perplexities of the world with nothing more than a tentative moral code which he is at liberty to revise as he sees fit. How do you distinguish this beautiful theory from sheer moral anarchy?

MODERNIST: You have got to have some faith in the commonsense and decent instincts of your fellow men.

FUNDAMENTALIST: Have you such faith?

MODERNIST: Yes. Haven't you?

FUNDAMENTALIST: No. I haven't. Such a

faith is contradicted by that experience of mankind to which you are so fond of appealing. Your natural man is a natural barbarian, grasping, selfish, lustful, murderous. Your psychoanalysts will tell you that. The religious teachers knew it long before the psychoanalysts rediscovered it. They called it original sin. They knew man was unworthy until he had been redeemed, or as you would say, educated.

MODERNIST: And what does that prove?

FUNDAMENTALIST: That even if the modernists could agree upon a moral code, they could not inculcate morality. For the moral life is due not to the acceptance of a set of rules but to a transformation of the will.

MODERNIST: And what have you to offer that will transform the will except the kindly advice and the good example of the wise?

FUNDAMENTALIST: I have the knowledge that I am part of a universe governed by a divine plan to which, if I wish to be everlastingly happy, I must make my will conform.

MODERNIST: In order to be good is it necessary to believe all that? Have there not been good men who disbelieved it?

FUNDAMENTALIST: No doubt there have been. Yet you will not deny that the great mass of mankind has always insisted upon believing that it was in communion with, and subject to, a will greater than its own. Do you know of any popular morality in the history of the world which has not had some sort of supernatural sanction?

MODERNIST: I do not know of any popular morality. But I know that there have been men who lived nobly without supernatural sanction.

FUNDAMENTALIST: Is it your hope, then, that what a few men have done all men might ultimately do?

MODERNIST: That is, I suppose, the faith of the modernist.

FUNDAMENTALIST: Are you not rather an optimist?

MODERNIST: In what respect?

FUNDAMENTALIST: You admit that all history shows how few men have been able to live a moral life without the conviction that they were obeying a divine will. You then point out a few unusual men, a few stoics perhaps, a few Epicureans, a few followers of Spinoza, a few pure and disinterested spirits among the scientists, and you ask me to believe that what this trifling minority has achieved through innate moral genius, the great humdrum mass of mankind is to achieve by what you optimistically describe as education. I do not believe it.

MODERNIST: If I accepted your argument I should be forced to the conclusion that the mass of mankind are incapable of receiving the truth.

FUNDAMENTALIST: That horrifies you?

MODERNIST: It does indeed.

FUNDAMENTALIST: I thought you had solemnly sworn to follow the truth wherever it might lead. But when you are confronted with the possibility that mankind cannot receive truth, you shrink from that truth. Does that not rather tend to confirm my suggestion that the appetite for truth is not so strong after all?

MODERNIST: That is an ingenious paradox and I haven't time to unravel it. Come back to the main point. You were saying that only a small minority has ever found the moral life possible without the absolute assurance that it was obeying a divine will.

FUNDAMENTALIST: And you were admitting that the task of modernism is to teach the vast majority to live as only this small minority has previously lived. I was expressing my doubts as to whether the modernists would succeed.

MODERNIST: Are they not compelled to try?

FUNDAMENTALIST: I'll let you answer that.

MODERNIST: Then I should say that nothing can now arrest the penetration of the scientific spirit into every field of opinion. You do not seriously think your laws against Darwin and the rest are effective?

FUNDAMENTALIST: Apparently they are not.

MODERNIST: Then what you call unbelief—that is, disbelief that there exists an authoritative account of destiny—is bound to infect the whole population. That being the fact, is it not our task to prepare men to lead independent, rational lives?

FUNDAMENTALIST: I might grant you that unbelief is bound for the time to spread. But I cannot believe you will succeed in teaching the great mass of men to lead independent, rational lives.

MODERNIST: You believe that all men are the children of God?

FUNDAMENTALIST: I do. And that most of them are children.

MODERNIST: That they are endowed by their Creator with reason and conscience?

FUNDAMENTALIST: Yes.

MODERNIST: Why then deny to the humblest that salvation which some of the greatest have found?

FUNDAMENTALIST: You are argumentative, and you are very naïve.

MODERNIST: If there is one thing we modernists are not, it is naïve. We are highly sophisticated people.

FUNDAMENTALIST: I withdraw the word naïve. You are merely ignorant. You have never studied the history of religions. Naturally you are ignorant.

MODERNIST: I have studied the history of religions.

FUNDAMENTALIST: Then how could you have failed to observe that the greatest teachers, Jesus, St. Paul, Buddha, Plato, Spinoza, all of them, taught that the perfect life was too difficult for the mass of men, that it required discipline and renunciation which most men could not endure, that it was in fact beyond their moral capacities?

MODERNIST: You mean that 'narrow is the gate'?

FUNDAMENTALIST: I do. Spinoza said that the way of salvation must be hard or it would not be by almost all men neglected.

MODERNIST: What you are saying now seems to destroy what you were saying before. You began by asking me how you could convince your children that they should accept morality if they were not first convinced that it is God's will. Now you are saying that it is extremely difficult for most men to obey God's will.

FUNDAMENTALIST: The great religious teachers, my friend, reached up to heaven, but their feet were firmly planted upon the earth. They had no illusions, as you have, about the capacities of men. That is why every important religion contains every grade of teaching from the grossest superstition to the purest expression of the spirit. Nobody who examines Buddhism or Christianity can have the slightest doubt that they have been adapted in the course of time to all the different intellectual and moral levels of mankind.

MODERNIST: And what do you deduce from these rather broad and doubtful generalizations of yours?

FUNDAMENTALIST: I deduce the extremely important conclusion that modernists are trying to grow grapes from thistles. And that that is a rather naïve thing to do.

MODERNIST: I told you once that I objected to the word naïve.

FUNDAMENTALIST: Well, I don't know what to call it. But are you not in fact blithely proposing to teach the scientific method to a mass of people who haven't the remotest chance of understanding it?

MODERNIST: I said we were compelled to try because the supernatural systems of authority were ceasing to be credible in the modern world.

FUNDAMENTALIST: That you are helping to break down the supernatural systems of authority I won't deny. But that you are teaching men to do without them I am not so sure.

MODERNIST: Why should you be so doubtful? The western world was once pagan. Then it became Catholic. Then a part of it became Protestant. Why should it not now become scientific?

FUNDAMENTALIST: Because this last change calls for the profoundest change in the habits of the human mind which has ever taken place. It means that men must learn to act with certainty upon premises which are uncertain. Your scientific method cannot guarantee its conclusions beyond all shadow of doubt.

MODERNIST: Of course it cannot.

FUNDAMENTALIST: But the mass of men won't tolerate this much uncertainty. They are not sufficiently disinterested. They will make incontrovertible dogmas out of scientific hypotheses. You are not teaching science when you teach a child that the earth moves around the sun rather than, as the Bible teaches, that the sun moves around the earth.

MODERNIST: I know that.

FUNDAMENTALIST: So that what your scientific education comes down to is this. A minority, perhaps a slowly growing minority acquire the scientific habit of mind and learn to live the disinterested kind of life which science demands. But the rest merely acquire odds and ends of more or less obsolete information which, while it destroys the authority and the majesty of their inherited religion, is in itself morally worthless. It fits into no plan, it supports no ideal of life. It provides no background for the human spirit.

MODERNIST: I find all this rather depressing.

FUNDAMENTALIST: I remind you again that as a modernist you are a devotee of the truth.

MODERNIST: What truth are you talking about?

FUNDAMENTALIST: A truth which shatters many pretences and illuminates some of the confusion of the modern mind.

MODERNIST: I am all agog to hear this truth.

FUNDAMENTALIST: Then you shall hear it. In our public controversies you are fond of arguing that you are open-minded, tolerant and neutral in the face of conflicting opinions. That is not so. You are fond of arguing that the conclusions of science can be reconciled with the conclusions of theology. That is evasive. These claims deceive nobody. They are merely adopted as convenient pretences by the politically minded, the timid, and the superficial. You know and I know that the issue is not whether Adam was created at nine o'clock in the morning or whether he descended from an ape. The issue is whether there exists a Book which, because it is divinely inspired, can be regarded by men as the "infallible rule of faith and practice," or whether men must rely upon human reason alone, and henceforth do without an infallible rule of faith and practice. What you challenge is not Genesis but revelation, and what I am defending ultimately is the faith of men that they know the Word of God.

I would ask you therefore not to be confused by the incidental ignorance of your partisans and of mine. It is of no consequence in itself whether the earth is flat or round. But it is of transcendent importance whether man can commune with God and obey His directions, or whether he must trust his own conscience and reason to find his way through the jungle of life. On that question it is impossible for an honest man to be neutral. It is impossible for him to be tolerant. It is impossible for him to be open-minded.

MODERNIST: I don't see that.

FUNDAMENTALIST: You can say: Maybe Darwin is right . . . maybe Lamarck is right . . . perhaps Einstein is right . . . perhaps he isn't. . . . That is your scientific spirit. But you can't say: Perhaps the word of God is right and perhaps it isn't.

MODERNIST: Why can't you?

FUNDAMENTALIST: Because the authority of the Bible rests upon revelation, and if you are open-minded about revelation you simply do not believe in it. Doubt is an essential part of the method of science, but it is the negation of faith. To say that you are open-minded about the inspiration of the Bible is nonsense. Open-mindedness in this connection is a perfectly definite rejection of the Bible's inspiration.

MODERNIST: I don't understand.

FUNDAMENTALIST: What do you mean by open-mindedness?

MODERNIST: A refusal to reach a conclusion on the ground that the evidence is not conclusive.

FUNDAMENTALIST: Exactly. But those who believe in the divine authority of the Bible believe it on grounds which are beyond the reach of human inquiry and evidence. Once you subject that authority to the test of human reason you have denied the essence of its authority. You have made the finite understanding the judge of the infinite. You are then, in the historic meaning of the word, an unbeliever.

MODERNIST: Is there no way out of this conflict?

FUNDAMENTALIST: That is not for me to say. I speak for the ancient and established order of mankind. You are the newcomer. You are the rebel. I do not know what you are going to do about it. You can disguise this issue but you cannot obliterate it.

MODERNIST: We can at least discuss it like gentlemen, without heat, without rancor.

FUNDAMENTALIST: Has it ever occurred to you that this advice is easier for you to follow than for me?

MODERNIST: How so?

FUNDAMENTALIST: Because for me an eternal plan of salvation is at stake. For you there is nothing at stake but a few tentative opinions none of which means anything to your happiness. Your request that I should be tolerant and amiable is, therefore, a suggestion that I submit the foundation of my life to the destructive effects of your skepticism, your indifference, and your good nature. You ask me to smile and to commit suicide. . . .

4. THOMPSON'S CIRCUS: THE BACKGROUND

I propose now to turn from the issues raised by Mr. Bryan's inquisition at Dayton to those raised by Mayor Thompson's inquisition at Chicago. I hope you will bear with me for I intend to consider Mayor Thompson's crusade seriously. I am well aware that much might be said about the sincerity of his crusade, and that we are confronted here with demagogy in the literal meaning of the term, with an agitator, that is to say, who has acquired influence with the populace by pandering to their prejudices and playing on their ignorance. I know, too, that Mayor Thompson is the head of a political machine which is greatly interested in contracts and in patronage. But after all that has been said, the fact remains that this demagogue has gotten hold of something which not only has a large popular appeal, but is sufficiently impressive to have overawed and silenced many educated men and women who detest it. It is especially significant, I think, that the criticism of Mayor Thompson has consisted almost entirely of derision at his tomfoolery and of attacks on his motives. There has been no very bold challenge of his premises. When he poses as a great patriot, he is attacked as a poseur. But little is said about the patriotism which he pretends to represent. There is an instinctive feeling that this is a delicate matter, about which it is not possible to say too much at the present time.

Now whatever we may think of his motives and his methods, it is necessary to recognize at once that this crusade did not originate in Chicago and is not confined to Chicago.[1] The crusade has taken form within the last ten years. It is a movement to preserve the patriotic tradition as to American relations with Great Britain. This tradition which arose out of the struggle of the revolting colonies has naturally been anti-British.

In 1917 the United States for the first time in its history became the associate of Great Britain in a great war. A part of the American people objected openly to this association. A still larger part, while they did their duty loy-

[1] *Cf.* Bessie Louise Pierce, *Public Opinion and the Teaching of History in the United States;* Harold Underwood Faulkner, "Perverted American History," in Harper's Magazine, February, 1926.

ally, nevertheless detested the war, and believed
in their hearts that the United States had been
inveigled into it by the cleverness of British
diplomats. The patriotic tradition which they
had learned from their school textbooks dis-
posed them to suspect all political contact with
Great Britain.

To offset this latent distrust of our associate
in the war, a great corps of historians was mo-
bilized, partly under government auspices, who
proceeded then and there to revise the whole
American historical tradition by obliterating
and explaining away the memories of the Revo-
lutionary War. This willingness on the part
of well known historians to manufacture a new
patriotic tradition to suit the political necessi-
ties of 1917 was resented. The prestige of
scholarship was injured. It was made plain
that history is something that can be cut and
shaped to suit the purposes of the moment.

Nevertheless, in the wake of these propa-
gandist historians there came a school of criti-
cal and honest historians. Once the authority
of the patriotic legends had been dissolved, the
opportunity of the critical historians presented
itself. American school history, particularly
in its bearing upon Anglo-American relations,
began to be rewritten, first by those who wished

to create a new, a pro-British legend, and then by those who wished to do away with all legends and to tell the truth which objective research had found.

After the war was over, after the peace treaty had been rejected, after the country had violently reverted to normalcy, the popular reaction against the revision of the patriotic legends got under way. No distinction was made, of course, between the revision carried out as propaganda in the interest of the Allies, and the revision carried out by scholars in the interest of the truth. In 1921 the whole heresy was set forth in a series of syndicated articles written by Mr. Charles Grant Miller. He exposed what he described as the "organized policy of propitiation toward Great Britain," and his exposure was widely circulated as a pamphlet under the title *Treason to American Tradition: the Spirit of Benedict Arnold Reincarnated*. This was the clarion call of patriotic fundamentalism.

There was a rally at once not only by those who had a single-hearted devotion to the American tradition, but also by those who might reasonably be described as having a single-hearted dislike of Great Britain. The charges against the new textbooks were taken up by such diverse organizations as the Sons of the American Revolution, the Daughters of the American Revolution, the Descendants of the Signers of the Declaration of Independence, the Knights of Columbus, the Knights of the Ku Klux Klan, the New Jersey Council of the Junior Order of United Mechanics, the American Legion, the Knights of Pythias, the German societies and the American Federation of Labor. In New York City the Board of Education investigated its textbooks, and Mayor John F. Hylan of New York had another uproarious investigation of his own. The same proceedings in one form or another were gone through in cities as far apart as Boston, Mass., and Portland, Oregon. Several states, New York, Wisconsin and Oregon, passed laws designed to do for patriotic fundamentalism what the Tennessee statute had been designed to do for religious fundamentalism.

By this time the situation had become very much confused. There were the old-fashioned textbooks which without self-consciousness set forth the old legends. There were the new propagandist books written to cement the friendship of the English-speaking peoples. There were the self-conscious and synthetic books written to restore the old traditions.

There were the new objective, critical books written by men with no axe to grind. And then on top of all this came the new bold school of debunking historians who exploited what the scholars had discovered and created out of it a cult of irreverence. They wrote elaborate treatises about the clay feet of the idols.

Amidst all these attacks and counter-attacks, the Council of the American Historical Association recently set forth its position in resolutions which state that

> genuine and intelligent patriotism, no less than the requirement of honest and sound scholarship, demand that textbook writers and teachers should strive to present a truthful picture of past and present, with due regard to the different purposes and possibilities of elementary, secondary and advanced instruction; that *criticism of history textbooks should, therefore, be based not upon grounds of patriotism, but only upon grounds of faithfulness to fact as determined by specialists, or tested by consideration of the evidence.* [Italics mine.]

This is the ideal of the critical scholar. It is in conflict with the ideal of many important sections of the American people. The American Legion, for example, in a very moderate report, says that the proper school history not only must be truthful but must "Speak Warmly . . . Have Enthusiasm . . . Preserve the Legends . . . Praise Noble Deeds . . . Encourage Faith . . . Build High Self Respect . . . Emphasize Effort and Success, not Failure." Plainly there are here two different conceptions of the teaching of history in the schools. The scholars stand squarely upon the principle that history books are to be judged "not upon grounds of patriotism, but only upon grounds of faithfulness to fact." The Legion, which stands for the popular belief, insists that the truth be taught with primary regard for its effect upon the morals and patriotism of the pupils.

5. DIALOGUE AT CHICAGO

AMERICANIST: I don't care for these isms. Couldn't I be called a plain one-hundred percent American?

SCHOLAR: I'm afraid not. That would be begging the question we are here to discuss.

AMERICANIST: And that question is what?

SCHOLAR: Whether as Archbishop Whately once remarked truth is to be put in the first place or in the second. I maintain that a sound patriotism must rest upon truthful history, and you maintain, I believe, that only a sound patriotism can determine what is true history.

AMERICANIST: That's about it. I don't believe the historians know what they mean when they say the criticism of history textbooks should be based only upon grounds of faithfulness to fact. What facts, for example, ought they to be faithful to?

SCHOLAR: Those which are determined by specialists and tested by the consideration of evidence.

AMERICANIST: The facts about any historical event are very numerous, are they not?

SCHOLAR: Very numerous indeed.

AMERICANIST: All the facts about George Washington, for example, would include the facts about his ancestry, his education, his character, his social position, his income, his political connections, his personal relations, as well as the chronicle of public events in which he participated. His conduct at any particular juncture must have been the resultant of very complex forces. Do you describe all these forces in your textbooks?

SCHOLAR: That is obviously impossible. There are too many, and some are obscure. It is necessary to select the significant ones.

AMERICANIST: And by what criterion do you select the significant ones?

SCHOLAR: That depends on the historian's philosophy of history. There are a number of schools of historical writing.

AMERICANIST: Such as——

SCHOLAR: There is a school which lays particular emphasis on the influence of great men. That is a bit old-fashioned today. There is a school which emphasizes the racial factor, and another which emphasizes the economic, and another the social, and another the ideological.

AMERICANIST: Which of these is the true history?

SCHOLAR: That depends on which school you belong to.

AMERICANIST: Well which ought to be taught in the public schools?

SCHOLAR: They ought all to have a hearing, that is, all the important ones.

AMERICANIST: Then history is not a very exact science.

SCHOLAR: It can be studied in a scientific spirit.

AMERICANIST: By the pupils as well as by the historian?

SCHOLAR: Yes, though for the very young children history must be taught as a story. In the upper grades mere story-telling ought to give way to a critical and skeptical examination.

AMERICANIST: What is the purpose of this?

SCHOLAR: In the words of the Council of the American Historical Association: "The cultivation in pupils of a scientific temper in history and the related social sciences, of a spirit of inquiry and a willingness to face unpleasant facts are far more important objectives than the teaching of special interpretations of particular events."

AMERICANIST: Then your purpose is not to teach the pupils a true account of American history but to teach them to have an inquiring state of mind?

SCHOLAR: Exactly.

AMERICANIST: You don't want them to believe whole-heartedly in any version of history?

SCHOLAR: No. They should learn to suspend judgment, to be open-minded, and to realize the complexity of human affairs.

AMERICANIST: You do not want history used as a means of teaching patriotism?

SCHOLAR: The most desirable kind of patriotism is grounded in the scientific temper.

AMERICANIST: But the scientific temper exists in Germany and England and Japan and Norway. Does it produce American patriots in those countries?

SCHOLAR: The scientific temper does not produce patriots. It civilizes them.

AMERICANIST: But you have to produce the patriots before you can civilize them. How do you propose to do that if history is not to be taught as an account of the glorious achievements of our country? Can you make patriots of children by telling them that maybe Washington was right and maybe he wasn't, and that you don't know whether the War of 1812 was worth fighting or not, and that perhaps the speculators had too much to say in the first Congress?

SCHOLAR: Patriotism does not depend upon illusions. It does not depend upon untruth. You don't exalt it very much by insisting that it can't survive the telling of the truth. I think better of it than that.

AMERICANIST: Well, suppose you tell me just what patriotism is.

SCHOLAR: Primarily, I suppose, it is love of the place where you were born, a kind of profound unreasoning affection for the landmarks of your childhood. And then it is a mystical identification of yourself with the destiny of the people to whom you belong,—a sense that your life is part of a larger life which is the life of your people.

AMERICANIST: That is not bad. I can see that your heart is in the right place.

SCHOLAR: Thank you. I also have a head, which I hope is in the right place.

AMERICANIST: Then why don't you use your head? Your definition of patriotism is admirable. It more than justifies all I have been contending for.

SCHOLAR: Then there must be something wrong with my definition.

AMERICANIST: No. There is nothing wrong with it. You said that patriotism was primarily an affection for the landmarks of your childhood. Have you forgotten that millions of American citizens passed their childhood in Europe? Have you forgotten that many more millions of American citizens have moved all over the map since their childhood, and no longer have any place they can love? And have you forgotten that for those who haven't moved, and who might remain attached to landmarks, the landmarks themselves have been moved away, generally to make room for gas stations, garages, and great rabbit warrens with steam heat and a chorus of radio loud speakers? If patriotism is primarily an attachment to one's own origins, then I tell you American patriotism is weak at the roots.

SCHOLAR: Perhaps that is why it is so vociferous at the top.

AMERICANIST: Perhaps. But let me proceed. You said further that patriotism was a mystical identification of yourself with the destiny of the people to whom you belong. What is the American destiny? Do you know?

SCHOLAR: That is something we are now engaged in working out.

AMERICANIST: And all of our citizens are to engage in working out?

SCHOLAR: Yes.

AMERICANIST: And they, or millions of them at least, are without the primary affections which make up true patriotism. Doesn't that make you a bit nervous?

SCHOLAR: I'm nervous about a good many things. What can you do about it?

AMERICANIST: I can at least see to it that every child passing through the public schools has the same consciousness of what this country has done and has meant in the past. Then when these children grow up they may start from the same premises in working out the destiny of America.

SCHOLAR: Aren't you attempting to create a sort of synthetic patriotism?

AMERICANIST: Where the materials to make

the genuine article are lacking you have to look around for substitutes. The children of the Americanized will be Americans.

SCHOLAR: Truth then must yield precedence to Americanization?

AMERICANIST: You have already admitted that there is no such thing as true history. All history is an interpretation.

SCHOLAR: I may have admitted too much.

AMERICANIST: You also admitted that what you wanted was to cultivate the scientific temper, not to teach true history.

SCHOLAR: And what you want is to make sure that people will identify themselves with their country.

AMERICANIST: Yes. Doubt is a luxury. Open-mindedness is a luxury. They are excellent. They are admirable—in men who will instinctively do the right thing.

SCHOLAR: The right thing?

AMERICANIST: Skepticism is admirable in a man of honor. It's the very dèvil in a scoundrel. It simply makes him utterly unscrupulous about inventing reasons for what he wishes to do.

SCHOLAR: Why do you trust a skeptic if he is a gentleman and a man of honor?

AMERICANIST: Because I know what he will

do, regardless of how much he may fuss about his reasons for doing the honorable thing. When you set out to educate millions what matters fundamentally is not their capacity to reason. . . . I take leave to question that capacity, and to doubt whether you will ever produce a scientifically minded population. What counts is that their unconscious attachments and prejudices should be simple and loyal.

SCHOLAR: And not that they should be truthful?

AMERICANIST: You might make patriots of the mass of men. But have you any reason whatever for thinking that you can make critical scholars of them?

6. NOTE

We may break off the discussion at this point. I have made out the strongest case which I know for the fundamentalist in religion and in politics who is at war with the new scientific spirit in education. I propose in our next lecture to try to see if, in the light of these arguments, it is possible to define somewhat more clearly the function and the status of a teacher in the public schools.

Chapter III

The Teacher and the Rule of Majorities

III—*The Teacher and the Rule of Majorities*

I. IRRECONCILABLE CONFLICT

Until fairly recent times the rôle of the teacher was clearly defined. There existed a body of knowledge and certain well-established methods of thought which it was his task to transmit to the new generation. Essentially the ideal of education was that the child should acquire the wisdom of the elders. There were, no doubt, fierce disputes among the sects as to what was knowledge and what was error. But it was an accepted fact that in Catholic communities the child should learn Catholic dogma, that in Lutheran communities he should learn Lutheranism, that in Calvinistic communities he should learn Calvinism.

The growth of science has radically altered all this. For the ancient notion that there exists a completed body of knowledge, there has been substituted the notion of a growing and changing body of knowledge which is forever tentative and forever incomplete. Consequently, wherever science is the accepted mode of

83

thought, the ideal of education must be, not that the child shall acquire the wisdom of his elders, but that he shall revise and surpass it. The child is not taught to believe. He is taught to doubt and to inquire, to guess, to experiment, and to verify. The teacher no longer pretends to transmit wisdom. Instead he strives to develop wise habits.

The scientific spirit now dominates the intellectual classes of the western world. They do not always obey it faithfully or successfully, especially where their material interests are involved. But they acknowledge that the scientific spirit ought to prevail in all fields of human knowledge, and the teacher, in so far as he is intellectually responsible, must consider himself bound by the code of science. In the scientific method he must find the only true and final allegiance of his mind.

But as a man and as a citizen the teacher is under contract to the state. He is in fact a subordinate official of the state, and in the state the sovereign power resides, not in the community of scholars, but in a majority of the voters. Now in this phase of history it is by no means certain that a majority of the voters understand the scientific ideal of the scholar or will tolerate it when they see the consequences of its application. The older method of thought still survives in great sections of the people, and they are by no means prepared to abandon their beliefs, or to adopt the newer method of holding beliefs and of arriving at them. The teacher therefore finds himself living at a time of transition from one kind of thinking to another. He is the servant of a community which is in part fundamentalist in its mode of thought and in part modernist. His intellectual duty is to modernism, that is to say, to the belief that the human reason has the last word. But politically, economically, legally, he is subject to the orders of those who may believe that the preservation of the ancient fundamentalism either in religion or in nationalism is the first duty of man.

Those who wish to evade this issue are fond of saying that reason and free inquiry are neutral and tolerant of all opinions. That, as we have seen, cannot be the case. Reason and free inquiry can be neutral and tolerant only of those opinions which submit to the test of reason and free inquiry. But towards any opinion for which the claim is made that it rests on some other method of verification than reason's own, reason is of necessity either partisan and intolerant, or indifferent. What cannot be tested by the method of science, reason will either ignore

or reject. Carry reason and free inquiry to the
utmost limits of their tolerance : what can they
say to fundamentalism except that they are pre-
pared to inquire whether there is reasonable
evidence for believing that the tests of reason
are not reliable ?

The disagreement goes to the very premises
of thought, to the character of thinking itself.
It revolves upon the question of whether human
reason is or is not the ultimate test of truth for
men. The fundamentalist cannot admit that it
is. He would cease to be a fundamentalist if he
were no longer convinced that above human
reason and the available evidence there is a gos-
pel which contains a statement of facts that are
the fundamental premises of all reasoning. His
belief that there exists such a gospel certifies his
opinions absolutely for him. He must conclude
that where our reason contradicts these opin-
ions, it is a sign not that the opinions are wrong,
but that our senses have deceived us or that we
have reasoned wrongly.

To ask the fundamentalist, therefore, to sub-
mit his belief to scientific inquiry is to ask him
at the outset to surrender the most important
attribute of his faith. It is evasive to tell him
that science may after investigation confirm his
opinion, or that it is possible to invent a formula

which will reconcile his belief with the conclusions of science. The conclusions of science are radically different from the conclusions of the fundamentalist even when there is a nominal or superficial agreement between them. They are certified by different systems of thought. The effect, therefore, of asking the fundamentalist to approach the tribunal of reason is to ask him to accept the jurisdiction of a court which is not his own. It is asking him to say that while that which has been revealed may be true, it is not true because it is revealed.

2. THE NEUTRALITY OF THE TEACHER

Since the conflict between fundamentalism and modernism is essentially irreconcilable, the teacher who wishes to understand his position in the modern state must abandon the notion that he is a neutral. It is impossible for him or for anyone else to be neutral. In so far as he makes any impression whatsoever on his pupils he must tend either to confirm or to weaken the ancient modes of thinking; he must lead the child either toward the modern spirit or away from it.

Had he taught two hundred years ago he would hardly have been conscious of this dilemma anywhere in the western world. There are still vast communities where the ancient ways are still so strong that the teacher need make no choice.   There are some communities on the other hand, not many as yet, I think, where the new ways are already firmly established.   There the teacher is not faced with this problem.   But in most communities in America today the old ways survive powerfully, either in religion or in nationalism, and yet the new ways are already powerful and insistent.   The teacher in such communities is in genuine difficulties.   And the more spirited and sensitive he is, the more profound those difficulties are likely to be for him.

I would not attempt to give teachers so situated advice as to how to conduct themselves even if I knew what advice to give them.   For it is evident that any teacher who is capable of realizing his position in the modern state is also capable of deciding how he will conduct himself in the light of the exact circumstances in his particular case.   The choice of a line of conduct is his personal affair, and I shall have failed altogether in these lectures if I have not at least suggested the complexity and the risks of the transition in which the teacher occupies so responsible a place.   For the introduction of modern habits of thought into the schools means a widening of the breach between the older generation and the younger.   It means that parents and children may come to think so differently that neither can sympathize with or even comprehend the other. It means a dissolution of codes and rules which rest upon the ancient foundations. It means dangerous and bewildering experiment, not only in thought, but in action, and there is no certainty that any experiment will work out happily.

But while I do not know how far any particular teacher ought to go in evoking the doubts, the inquiries, and the experiments of modernism, of this at least I am certain: that the more clearly the teacher realizes the nature of this transition and its profound implications, the more successfully he will find his way through its perplexities. If he knows what he is doing, he will know better what to do. His predecessors were the custodians of a temple. But he belongs to a generation which amidst great hesitation, wild hope and deep fear, is engaged in taking down the stones of the temple and in erecting something new, of which the plan is not quite clear, in its place. If he imagines that the ancient temple is still intact he is hugging an illusion. If he acts on the assumption that the new structure is wholly erected, he will soon discover his error. Only by understanding that he is in the midst of a revolutionary change, and that he is a responsible agent of that change, can he hope to find out what his duty is.

3. BRIDGES FOR THE UNLEARNED

The statement that the teacher today is a responsible agent of the change from the fundamentalist to the scientific method of thought leads, I think, to certain inferences which may clarify his position somewhat more. He is, let us remember, a teacher. He is not, let us remember, engaged in research to extend the boundaries of human knowledge. As a teacher he stands somewhere between the unlearned and immature on the one hand and the learned and the mature on the other. He has, therefore, to take into account not merely the correct science of his time but the minds and characters of his pupils.

Were he a scholar he could disregard entirely the ignorance of his pupils. He would address himself only to the problem under investigation, caring nothing who understood him or what impression he created. But being a teacher he is concerned primarily not with the discovery of truth but with its reception. He cannot merely announce the truth. He must communicate it. Because he must communicate it, he must take into account not merely what it is desirable to communicate but what it is possible to communicate.

If all the pupils in America could be present at meetings of learned societies where new discoveries are announced, the mere fact that they heard the words would not constitute education. For when the pupils heard these announcements, few of them would hear more than so many vocables. These vocables have significance only for those who can attribute significance to them. In the scientific announcement a whole chain of meanings and of previous agreements is taken for granted. It is assumed, for example, that the audience knows the vocabulary and the grammar which the scientist employs, that it knows the logical processes on which he relies, that it is aware of the history and meaning of the problem with which the new discovery deals. I am, for example, unable to appreciate Einstein's work. I do not know the meaning of the words and the symbols he employs. I cannot follow his mathematical processes. Above all I am too ignorant of physics to realize what it was that was inadequate in the Newtonian physics which raised the problems Einstein set himself to solve. If I, therefore, were to take up the study of Einstein's work, I should need to start far behind where Einstein began.   I

should need someone who not only understands
Einstein, but also understands my ignorance,
who knows not only what Einstein has dis-
covered, but what I have not yet discovered,
someone who can begin where my pitiably in-
adequate training ends and will with patience
and ingenuity build a bridge for me. I need a
teacher.

An adequate science would, of course, in-
clude not only Einstein's physics, but a knowl-
edge of the ignorance, the stupidity, the preoc-
cupations and the indifference, which prevent me
from understanding Einstein's physics.   The
study of human ignorance is a science, a branch
of psychology, on which all those who teach, in
schools, in pulpits, in print, are compelled to
draw. They are good teachers in so far as they
are adepts in human ignorance, and skilful in
dealing with it. I say skilful, because the manip-
ulation of human ignorance cannot be reduced
to cut and dried methods. The particular qual-
ity of the ignorance of each individual is a
unique combination which can be dealt with suc-
cessfully only by those whose general under-
standing is quickened by intuitive sympathy. The
great journalist has this flair. The great orator
has it. It is a sense of the audience, an aware-
ness of the dim attitudes of those who are

listening. And the only difference between what we call demagoguery and honest teaching, is that the demagogue exploits the ignorance of his audience by solidifying it behind purposes that cannot be rationally defended, whereas the teacher is always trying to dissolve the ignorance of his audience by leading them to discover for themselves purposes that will stand the test of reason.

The true teacher is not concerned with persuading his hearers to accept his conclusion rather than their own. He is concerned with the rationalization of the process by which conclusions are reached. For that reason the teacher in a time of transition like the one amidst which we live, must make the transition itself the subject matter of his teaching. He does not do his work if he teaches fundamentalism. He does not do his work if he teaches modernism. He is a teacher only if he teaches the transition from fundamentalism to modernism.

I am persuaded that the failure to realize this situation accounts for many of the quarrels which come to public attention under the rubric of quarrels about the freedom of teaching. It does not account for all of the quarrels. There are, I am sure, many cases where scholars have been subjected to interference by the authorities who, out of prejudice or self-interest, object to their following out certain lines of inquiry.   But I am not speaking here of scholars.   I am speaking of teachers, and my own impression is that very frequently the difficulty arose because the teacher had failed to teach, and had insisted, sometimes rather provocatively, on announcing strange and unpalatable doctrines which he held to be the truth.   The teacher who was in trouble had forgotten, or he had shirked, the tedious and difficult business of building a bridge from the ignorance of his pupils to the knowledge which he was trying to give them.

4. CONCERNING PRUDENCE

If the teacher had only to consider his pupils, these comments might be roughly sufficient. But of course the teacher is compelled to consider not only the state of mind of his pupils but the wishes of their parents.   If he is an employee of the state, he is under orders from officials, who in their turn derive their authority from the voters.   The teacher cannot teach these voters.   He cannot build bridges for them. They constitute a force to which he must somehow accommodate himself.   They hold the purse strings.   They are the sovereign

power. The final question then is: what shall
be the philosophy of a modern teacher towards
his employers and his sovereign, the reigning
majority of the voters?

When I speak of philosophy I mean: what
ought he to think of the opinions and wishes of
the majority? Of what he should do in the
light of what he thinks, each man must again
be his own judge in the light of the particular
circumstances. Nobody can lay down a general
rule as to what another John T. Scopes ought
to do,—whether he ought to resign, or to fight,
or to evade the issue. At least I cannot say it,
because I do not think it is very good taste to
advise other men whether or not they ought to
be martyrs.

It would surely be very bad taste in a
newspaperman, for no newspaper of large cir-
culation can possibly represent the full, candid,
unhesitating mind of its editors. They are
compelled almost every day to weigh the ad-
vantages and disadvantages of candor, and to
strike a prudent balance on which they act. I
am telling no secrets. There are editors who do
not have to be prudent because they have no im-
prudent opinions. There are editors who do
not have to be prudent, because they have no
readers whom they have to conciliate. There

are editors who have to be prudent not to offend the majority, and there are editors who have to be prudent not to offend the minority. But prudence is an element in the judgment of every editor who has a following, the most liberal and the most conservative. Though timidity often makes it excessive, wherever men are bent upon persuading and influencing other men, some prudence in respect to their prejudices is necessary to success.

The question then is not how prudently the teacher ought to act in the presence of the will of the majority, but what weight he should inwardly give to it. When he is clear as to that, he is in no danger of confusing his timidity, his convenience, and his ambitions, with a just prudence.

5. DIALOGUE IN AMERICA: CONCERNING MAJORITY RULE

I shall suppose that the teacher finds himself in a community like Dayton or Chicago, where an effective majority of the voters is insisting that he shall make the schools safe for some kind of fundamentalism.

SOCRATES: The question you are asking yourself is what respect you ought to have in your own mind for the wishes of a majority. What then do you mean by wishes?

TEACHER: I mean the wish that in teaching science I shall not impugn revelation and that in teaching history I shall not impugn tradition.

SOCRATES: You being yourself one who accepts the authority of reason?

TEACHER: Yes.

SOCRATES: Then you cannot accept the authority of revelation or of tradition?

TEACHER: No. But I am employed by people a majority of whom do accept it.

SOCRATES: Have you complete confidence in reason?

TEACHER: In reason, yes.—In my reasoning, no.

SOCRATES: You feel that you may be wrong, and that the majority may be right.

TEACHER: Surely that is possible.

SOCRATES: Do you feel that the opinions of the majority may be right because they are the opinions of the majority?

TEACHER: Sometimes. But not always. The difficulty is to know when. There is some kind of wisdom in numbers.

SOCRATES: Your task then is to find out, if you can, what kind of wisdom there is in numbers.

TEACHER: Yes. It is plain, I think, that the majority is often wrong. It is equally plain that the educated minority has often been wrong.

SOCRATES: Then perhaps being right or wrong has nothing to do with majorities and minorities.

TEACHER: I am not satisfied with that. There are times, I believe, when an opinion is entitled to particular respect because it is the opinion of the majority.

SOCRATES: It would have to be the kind of opinion about which the majority was competent to have an opinion. Would it not?

TEACHER: Obviously.

SOCRATES: Is the majority competent to have an opinion about physics and biology?

TEACHER: I am sure it is not. You cannot settle scientific controversies by the election returns.

SOCRATES: But you settle great human problems by the election returns. And these problems are more important in your lives than any problem in physics or biology.

TEACHER: We do not settle great human problems by the election returns. We find out which party is the stronger. We decide between two or more courses of action.

SOCRATES: Then what you can learn from

the majority is what the majority intends to do or consents to have done.

TEACHER: That is about what political democracy amounts to. Power today resides in numbers. It is necessary, therefore, for governments to satisfy numbers.

SOCRATES: Regardless of whether the majority is right or wrong?

TEACHER: In government it is necessary to know what the majority wants and what it will tolerate before you can know what is right or wrong. To act without that is to invite revolution.

SOCRATES: Then what the majority knows is what the majority wants. The people are experts on the subject of their own desires.

TEACHER: Not so very expert at that. They often do not know what they want. Less often do they know what they will want.

SOCRATES: Is it not so that they at least know at any particular moment what they think they want?

TEACHER: That much not even Mr. Mencken would deny.

SOCRATES: Pardon me, did I hear you say "Mr. Mencken"? I haven't met him.

TEACHER: A charming fellow, I assure you. You'll meet him soon.

SOCRATES: Then he is still alive,—but failing?

TEACHER: Yes. He can't last long, poor fellow. He is about to laugh himself to death. He has uncontrollable fits of merriment over his discovery that mankind is foolish.

SOCRATES: *His* discovery?

TEACHER: Well, he acts as if it were his discovery.

SOCRATES: It isn't.

TEACHER: I'm sorry I mentioned him. You never lived in America, so you cannot appreciate what a good man he is.

SOCRATES: Well, you did not have to mention him, did you?

TEACHER: I couldn't help it. I thought of him when you said the people know at any particular moment what they think they want.

SOCRATES: Does he admit that?

TEACHER: If he ever admitted anything, I think he would admit that.

SOCRATES: Do you think he 'would admit that the people know anything besides what they think they want?

TEACHER: God forbid that a poor pedagogue should speak for H. L. Mencken.

SOCRATES: He must be an awe-inspiring fellow. Well, what is the poor pedagogue prepared to admit here where H. L. Mencken can't bawl him out?

TEACHER: That the judgment of many men might at times be wiser than the judgment of a few men.

SOCRATES: Certainly. But what judgments?

TEACHER: Those in which racial instincts ought to play a part.

SOCRATES: Can you define that?

TEACHER: No, but I feel in my bones that there are many momentous things about which the sense of ordinary men may be more reliable than the opinions of experts and theorists.

SOCRATES: Can you not feel it in *your* bones when such a question has arisen?

TEACHER: The feelings in my bones are not so trustworthy as they were. They are confused by learning. I am analytical. I am self-conscious. I can no longer trust my bones.

SOCRATES: You have admitted that the opinions of the majority are absolutely reliable as to what the majority thinks it wants. You then go on and suggest that in various vague but important matters the intuitions of the majority may be wise. But you do not know what those matters are?

TEACHER: I don't.

SOCRATES: They could not be matters upon

which science has passed judgment after thorough investigation?

TEACHER: No.

SOCRATES: Then they must be matters upon which science has not passed judgment?

TEACHER: I think so.

SOCRATES: On these you are inclined to trust the judgment of the majority?

TEACHER: I am not wholly certain.

SOCRATES: Is the judgment of the majority upon these great unsettled questions always perfectly clear?

TEACHER: It is rarely perfectly clear. It is often difficult to know what the majority thinks.

SOCRATES: How is that?

TEACHER: Well, the judgment of the majority in one of the five counties of a city like New York may differ from the judgment of a majority in the whole city. This majority may differ from the majority in the whole state. The state's majority may differ from the nation's. The nation's may differ from that of mankind.

SOCRATES: Then when you speak of a majority you really have to say first how many are to be included in the count?

TEACHER: Yes, and there are many ways of arranging the population so as to get the result

you want.   It is known in politics as gerry-
mandering.

SOCRATES: Would you ascribe the same mys-
tic wisdom to any majority of any group no mat-
ter how it was gerrymandered?

TEACHER: That would make nonsense of the
whole idea.

SOCRATES: Then the group in which the opin-
ions of the majority are entitled to special re-
spect must be a particular sort of group?

TEACHER: Yes.

SOCRATES: Particular in what way?

TEACHER: It must not be an artificial politi-
cal grouping.

SOCRATES: Those are vague words.

TEACHER: This is a subtle idea.   I hardly
know how to define it.

SOCRATES: Well, remember that you were
looking for the occasions when you ought to
trust the commonsense of ordinary men.   Do
you not have to say then that they must be occa-
sions in which the common experience of ordi-
nary men is significant?

TEACHER: And then what?

SOCRATES: Must they not be occasions of
which all of the ordinary men you consult have
had experience?

TEACHER: I think so.

SOCRATES: Then the group whose majority you respect must be a group of men who are closely related to one another in the matter which interests them. A family's opinion about the concerns of that family. A village opinion about the concerns of that village. A city's opinion about the concerns of that city.

TEACHER: When you get to the city I am not so sure. If you went on to a nation I'd be even less sure.

SOCRATES: Why is that?

TEACHER: Because in a city and in a nation there is little direct common experience. Most of the common experience is vicarious and deals with invisible matters uncertainly reported.

SOCRATES: The factor of error and deception enters?

TEACHER: All manner of illusion and what people now call propaganda.

SOCRATES: What is propaganda?

TEACHER: The art of controlling judgment by provoking false images to awaken prejudices.

SOCRATES: You call it an art.

TEACHER: One of the most potent in the modern world.

SOCRATES: To what do you ascribe its potency?

TEACHER: To the fact that mankind now lives in a society which is so large that no man can see much of it. We are all dependent upon others for our knowledge of this society. We have not yet learned how to make that knowledge trustworthy. This is the propagandist's opportunity.

SOCRATES: The propagandist can, I suppose, assemble majorities.

TEACHER: He can and he does.

SOCRATES: And to such majorities you do not wish to give any respect whatever?

TEACHER: I do not wish to, but I can't always help myself. Often it is not possible, moreover, to know whether the majority speaks a real judgment or repeats what propagandists have told it.

SOCRATES: The majorities which are drawn from large and more or less artificial groups are the least respectable.

TEACHER: They are the most powerful.

SOCRATES: We are not discussing power. We are discussing wisdom.

TEACHER: Then the opinions of the small homogeneous community in respect to its own concerns would be, I should say, the most respectable.

SOCRATES: Aristotle got as far as that.

TEACHER: We have not gotten much further.

SOCRATES: Your conclusion then is that this mystic wisdom of the people is most likely to appear in small groups dealing with their own affairs?

TEACHER: It is not likely to appear when they are dealing with other people's affairs, though most men seem to think so nowadays. And it is not likely to appear in large groups dealing with matters they know only by hearsay and can't very well understand. There can't be much wisdom in that.

SOCRATES: You are not, however, opposed to political democracy?

TEACHER: Am I opposed to the weather? On cold rainy days I am. The fact of democracy is as little subject to discussion in the modern world as the weather. Even dictators have to consult or cajole the people. There are two kinds of muddleheadedness in our own age on this question: there are the muddleheaded people who think the people are wise and the muddleheaded people who think they are foolish. Now Mr. Mencken——

SOCRATES: You were sorry the last time you mentioned him.

TEACHER: I won't mention him though it is

a little like trying not to think of a white elephant for ten consecutive minutes.

SOCRATES: You were not talking about Mr. Mencken or about white elephants. You were talking of muddleheaded people.

TEACHER: Yes, and I was about to say that they are muddleheaded because they judge democracy from the point of view of what is wise and of what is unwise, when as a matter of fact political democracy is a matter of finding out who intends to have the last word, and then of having the government behave accordingly.

SOCRATES: Then to the expressions of political democracy you give no inward respect whatever?

TEACHER: Ought I to?

SOCRATES: The majority is sovereign. Ought the sovereign not to be respected?

TEACHER: We have already discussed the difficulties, have we not?

SOCRATES: Yes, but your conclusion is a little puzzling. You have no inward respect for the opinions of most majorities. Can you obey a sovereign whose opinions you do not respect?

TEACHER: Can I serve that sovereign if I do respect his opinions?

SOCRATES: Never mind the paradoxes.

TEACHER: The relation of an individual to

democracy is a paradox. If everyone respected the opinions of the majority, those opinions would never improve. If everybody defied the opinions of the majority, there would be no government. And therefore no use in trying to improve the opinions of the majority.

SOCRATES: Your sovereign under democracy is a peculiar person.

TEACHER: He is not a person. He is many persons and not the same ones every day.

SOCRATES: Perhaps that is where your paradoxes arise. This democratic sovereign is not a person. It is a changing array of individuals. You may be part of the sovereign power one day and not the next.

TEACHER: Precisely.

SOCRATES: On the day when you are not part of it, you are one of the Outs hoping to become one of the Ins?

TEACHER: Or at least hoping to teach the Ins some better sense.

SOCRATES: Then whether you are out or in you are always helping to create the sovereign in a democracy?

TEACHER: In a manner of speaking.

SOCRATES: When you join the crowd you add to its force. When you resist the crowd, what happens to you?

TEACHER: I may lose my job. I may be pushed aside. I may be trampled upon.

SOCRATES: Is that the only fate of those who resist the crowd?

TEACHER: A very few become the leaders of the crowd.

SOCRATES: Is that all?

TEACHER: A few are cranks and fools.

SOCRATES: Is that all?

TEACHER: A few are martyrs and geniuses.

SOCRATES: What about those who go with the crowd. Are they all fools?

TEACHER: Certainly not.

SOCRATES: Are they all wise men?

TEACHER: Obviously not.

SOCRATES: Then to go with the crowd or against it is in itself no sign of wisdom or folly?

TEACHER: But we started out to see whether a man should respect or defy the crowd.

SOCRATES: And we have concluded that the majority is entitled to no particular respect. And that it is entitled to no particular disrespect. And that wise men may go with it. And that wise men may defy it. And that fools go with it. And that fools defy it. Is your question not answered?

TEACHER: How is it answered?

SOCRATES: Why, by saying that the rebellion

of a wise man is wise and that the rebellion of a fool is foolish.

TEACHER: I am not sure whether this is a paradox or a truism.

SOCRATES: It is neither. Whether a man shall conform or rebel is largely an accident of his temperament and his circumstances. But whether in his rebellion or conformity a man is wise or foolish, whether he knows what he is doing and why, and where he is going and how fast, and what the consequences are, what are the risks and the costs, what lies behind and ahead and in between—those are the questions on which everything depends.

TEACHER: Is there then no rule of conduct in these matters?

SOCRATES: Your Washington was willing to shed blood in order to defy the constituted authorities. Your Lincoln was willing to shed blood to uphold the constituted authorities. They have both been justified. There can be no rule of conduct. That which brave men do with wisdom lesser men make rules to justify.

6. A BROAD GENERALIZATION

To those who are seeking a simpler clue amidst these perplexities, I can offer only this suggestion: The advancement of human liberty has as a matter of practical politics consisted in building up centers of resistance against the absolutism of the reigning sovereign. For experience has shown that liberty is most ample if power is distributed, checked, and limited up to the point where it is paralyzed and is unable to maintain order. The struggles for liberty have consisted, therefore, in restraining the power of the Ins by the power of the Outs, in limiting the power of the king by the resistance of the nobles, or in limiting the power of the nobles by strengthening the power of the king. Whoever the sovereign, the program of liberty is to deprive him of arbitrary and absolute power.

In our age the power of majorities tends to become arbitrary and absolute. And therefore, it may well be that to limit the power of majorities, to dispute their moral authority, to deflect their impact, to dissolve their force, is now the most important task of those who care for liberty.

Chapter IV
Coda

IV—Coda

This attempt to explore the relationship between faith and reason and authority must end without a simple formulated conclusion. We have been dealing with variable and elusive ideas, with ancient habits of thought that are tentative and experimental, with notions like sovereignty and majority rule, which when they are examined turn out to be exceedingly elusive. Though the subject is in a sense one of the oldest problems which have perplexed men, the elements of it in its modern phase are strange. We have not known them long enough or well enough to reduce them to clear ideas. We are compelled still to fumble for words which will do justice to these meanings that we dimly perceive. It is no use pretending that we can as yet speak precisely and conclusively.

Perhaps the question is in the nature of things inconclusive. We speak of fundamentalism, of modernism, of tradition and criticism, of faith and science, of liberty and majority rule. But in the actual struggle there is no such thing as fundamentalism. There are only fundamentalists. Sincere fundamentalists and insincere. Men of simple and resolute faith. Men of conventional mind and indifferent. Brave and timid. Those who command respect. And those who invite derision. For the actual struggle the cause of science is in the hands of good scientists and stupid ones, of geniuses and quacks, disinterested men and men on the make. The struggle is confused by innumerable people who do not care, who are bored and preoccupied and uncomprehending. In the actual event we are not dealing with majority rule. We are dealing with shifting majorities, well led, badly led, instinctively right, bamboozled, assembled from day to day out of changing and uncertain human beings.

To reduce the conduct of all these individuals and the complex of their relationships to a logical pattern which can be discussed coherently and lectured about is a greater feat than we in this generation are likely to perform. We can explore. We can follow out the implications. We can become increasingly aware. But we cannot formulate and conclude. For in the whole confused struggle one factor is unpredictable and yet decisive. That is the human will. Logical analysis can clarify the will and the situation in which it operates. But logical analysis cannot anticipate what the human will is likely to make of the situation in which it finds itself. For us at least that must remain mysterious. For we do not understand, and therefore we cannot speak intelligently about, the creative activity of human beings.

Perhaps when the situation has developed further, is clearer and less novel, there will appear among us again men of genius, men with a surer instinct for reality than our own, with a more profound logic, and with the imagination to synthesize these ideas and make them orderly. Until that time comes,—if it comes, —we shall lack the support and the guidance of a philosophy. We shall live as we are now living without any sense of the whole, without any clear conception of our destiny, with only improvised ideas of what is the better and the worse. For us the words of William James are true: "There is no complete generalization, no total point of view, no all-pervasive unity, but everywhere some residual resistance to verbalization, formulation and discursification, some genius of reality that escapes from the pressure of the logical finger, that says 'Hands off,' and claims its privacy, and means to be left to its own life . . . what the intellect, with its claim to reason out reality, thinks that it is in duty bound to resolve . . . remains; but it remains as something to be met and dealt with by faculties more akin to our activities and heroisms and willingnesses, than to our logical powers."

All we can do in this generation is to begin to understand what it is that we need to understand more clearly. The tendencies of the situation in which we find ourselves have still to manifest them completely, and to ripen. We do not know the consequences of life in a society which is as vast and as intricate as our own. We do not know what the effect will be when the fundamentalism of mankind has been abandoned, not merely by the cultivated élite, but by great semi-literate aggregations of people. We are just emerging from a naïve and mystical conception of democracy. We are just becoming aware of the forces that are latent in masses of men who have been torn from the rule of custom and supernatural authority.

But we do know that since the Fourteenth Century in the Western World, a complex of forces has been at work dissolving the premises, the traditions, and the social ties which bound together the ancient order of human so-

ciety. These forces of dissolution have not yet exhausted themselves; they are penetrating the farthest corners of the world and the inner recesses of our souls.

Multitudes of men still live in communities that are isolated from this vast disturbance of modernity. They are untouched by doubt, and they live secure in conformity with their immemorial traditions. But in other places, which we have chosen to call the more advanced, the influences of modernity have begun to intrude. There is doubt, there is uncertainty, there is conflict between youth and age, between the contented and the unappeased. As men in their communities are drawn further into the orbit of change, the unsettlement of their habits increases. In this phase those who are appalled by the disturbance are likely to go fundamentalist in a kind of counter-reformation directed at the protestants and freethinkers. Dayton and Chicago belong to this phase. But the dissolution proceeds,—inexorably, I think —until at last the whole community is uprooted and modernized. But these moderns, though they are uprooted from the ancient foundations, retain many of the expectations of the ancient order of life. They crave certainty, they need guidance, they want compensations.

Wanting them they improvise them: they exalt majorities and constitutions, dictatorships, class interest and sectarian loyalties. They make endless laws, having lost the self-evident dominion of custom. They pursue the newest fad, lacking confidence in the older wisdom. They worship what is big, being uncertain what is good. They are beguiled by loud and clever words, having ceased to trust authority. They are excited nationalists because they are no longer attached to their homeland. They believe in the miracles of machinery and the messianic mission of science. They are unbelieving and credulous.

Here and there some have found a way of life in this new world. They have put away vain hopes, have ceased to ask guaranties, and are yet serene. But they are only a handful. They do the enduring work of the world, for work like theirs, done without ulterior bias and for its own sake, is work done in truth, in beauty, and in goodness. There is not much of it, and it does not greatly occupy the attention of mankind. Its excellence is quiet. But it persists through all the spectacular commotions. And long ages after, it is all that men care much to remember.

Breinigsville, PA USA
15 September 2009
224070BV00002B/5/P